SCOTLAND CAMPING

WITH KIDS

Scotland Camping with Kids
First published in the United Kingdom in 2011 by
Andrew Thomson – ScottishCamping.com Ltd,
Blairs College,
South Deeside Rd,
Aberdeen
AB12 5LF

www.ScottishCamping.com
Copyright © Andrew Thomson

A catalogue record of this book is available from the British Library.

ISBN: 978-0-9553049-3-4

While we have endeavoured to include full reviews on sites and recipes this has not always been possible and on several occasions these have had to be edited. All reviews are referenced to the contributors who have significantly added to the success of ScottishCamping.com and contributed to the production and relevance of *Scotland Camping with Kids*.

While substantial care and effort has been taken in the research of this book, ScottishCamping. com Ltd cannot accept any responsibility for any errors, omissions or inaccuracies. If any are found please feel free to contact us.

Edited by Anna Stevenson
Cover design and typesetting by Heather Macpherson, www.raspberryhmac.co.uk

Dedicated to Carolyn, Anna and Meg, my camping family, and to our ScottishCamping compatriots Alex, Hazel, Cameron, Rhona and Fifer

Introduction

Children love camping. Whether it's the initial night out in the back garden, a short weekend trip close by or a holiday week or two spent camping in Scotland, children will love it.

Camping with children is always fun and a fantastic way to get them away from modern living and back in touch with nature and the countryside. It is great for encouraging them to get plenty of fresh air and exercise while experiencing a different way of life and discovering and learning new skills. Camping helps children learn about life in a totally new environment and offers opportunities to share basic experiences, build relationships and create memories that last.

Fortunately for parents, camping has changed over the years. It has become a more convenient and comfortable experience than during their own childhood, thanks to the development of weatherproof, easy-to-put-up tents and modern sleeping materials to keep everyone warm.

Whether you intend camping in a tent, motorhome or caravan, camping with kids is now more than ever a great opportunity for families to share time and a wonderful way to discover all that Scotland has to offer.

Whether you are new to camping with children and don't really know where to start, or are just looking for new ideas for your nights under the stars, you have made the right choice by picking up this book. It provides essential information as well as numerous tips on a variety of camping topics including choosing equipment, setting up camp, what to cook and children's activities. It also features many of the best Scottish child-friendly sites and luckily for you and the kids this includes many of the world's best!

Imagine your perfect pitch: perhaps you are camping on a warm summer's evening on the edge of golden sands looking out on a glorious sunset over the Isles or at the edge of a gently lapping loch surrounded by majestic mountains.

With the aid of this book you can turn your vision into reality for the kids and can experience what has attracted people from all over the world to camp in Scotland and has inspired our own Scottish campers here for generations.

Don't just take our word for it, read on and see what other families say awaits your children on a camping trip!

Why camp in Scotland? Probably the best camping country in the world

Tourists travel to Scotland from around the globe to experience our stunning scenery, inspiring history, wonderful wildlife and world-famous hospitality.

Whether you live in Scotland or are a welcome visitor, this guide will offer you and your children information on a huge range of places to camp. Scotland has some of the world's best places for children to explore, fall asleep in or wake up to. This book will not tell you where to camp, like other guides do, but will instead describe many different types of sites in all corners of Scotland, leaving you to decide on your ideal destination. It recognises that you know your children best and what they want from their holiday and so you will find a variety of the most popular and child-friendly sites as reviewed by thousands of ScottishCamping.com website users.

Even if you do not wish to stay on official sites, Scotland allows you and your children to access and responsibly wild camp in more areas of outstanding natural beauty than any other country in Europe. If you wish to wild camp this book provides more information on this option.

If you are considering camping with children for the first time this book will help you take the plunge, even if it is just for a night to discover what you are missing. From this starting point we are sure you will be encouraged by the kids to take them camping more often. Camping really is the best way to get a sense for Scotland and will allow you and the children to savour the sights, sounds and smells of the great outdoors.

Camping can be a cheap holiday whether it is done in a planned or spontaneous way. A camping holiday will introduce your children to their own healthy, educational and unforgettable adventure. You may decide on a site close to home or further afield and there are many sites close to public transport. Nowadays you may also camp in a number of new ways and can even leave your tent at home and choose to have a camping experience in a wooden wigwam, yurt or pre-erected tent. Plan your meals and cook together, share your sleeping space and learn to socialise over a stove or open fire. This will provide a shared experience that you will all remember.

About the author

The author of this book, Andy Thomson, has been a camping enthusiast for many years. An occasional camper as a child, his enthusiasm began to develop during the early 1990s when he and his wife Carolyn camped extensively all over Scotland for recreation and holidays. Andy has also shared this enthusiasm for camping and the outdoors through his work with children which led to his undertaking a variety of outdoor qualifications and becoming a Summer Scottish Mountain Leader in 1991. Since this time he has led children and groups on many camping trips and outdoor activities in Scotland.

Spotting a significant gap in the camping information provided for outdoor enthusiasts and families, Andy, along with his camping friend Alex Barclay, set up ScottishCamping.com and have run the website for over a decade. Now with children of their own, camping has become a part of both of their families' lives. They have worked hard to establish their website as Scotland's most comprehensive camping and caravan park guide. It now lists over 500 official and unofficial campsites and has over 400,000 visitors every year. Alongside the campsite and caravan park directory the website also features their publications and reviews and photographs supplied by their site users, a busy message board and guidance on a variety of camping-related issues.

Scotland Camping with Kids has been compiled from ScottishCamping.com's extensive information database. Information has been sourced from the website, the camping map and directory and online reviews and tips supplied by our invaluable customer base. As a result ScottishCamping.com is now pleased to recommend to you the best sites for children as decided by Scotland's campsite users.

Contents

Map of sites

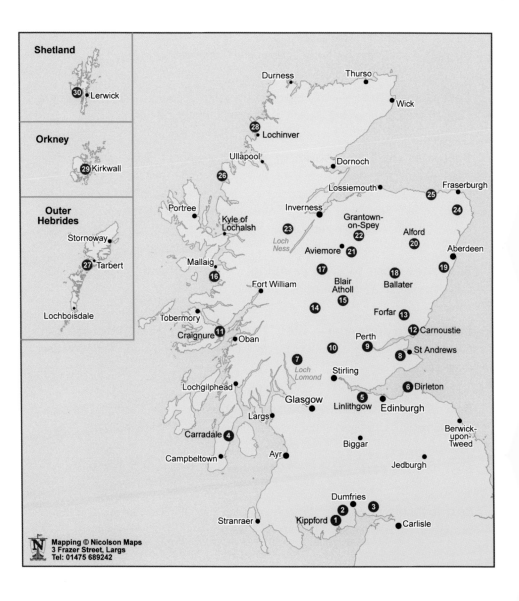

Shetland
30 Lerwick

Orkney
29 Kirkwall

Outer Hebrides
Stornoway
27 Tarbert
Lochboisdale

Durness
Thurso
Wick
28 Lochinver
Ullapool
Dornoch
26
Lossiemouth
Fraserburgh
Portree
25
24
Inverness
Kyle of Lochalsh
23
Grantown-on-Spey
Alford
22
Loch Ness
20
Aberdeen
Aviemore 21
Mallaig
19
16
17
Fort William
Blair Atholl
18 Ballater
15
14
Forfar 13
Tobermory
12 Carnoustie
Craignure 11
Oban
Perth
7
10
9
St Andrews
Loch Lomond
8
Stirling
Lochgilphead
6 Dirleton
Glasgow
5
Largs
Linlithgow
Edinburgh
Carradale 4
Berwick-upon-Tweed
Campbeltown
Ayr
Biggar
Jedburgh
Dumfries
2
3
Stranraer
Kippford 1
Carlisle

Mapping © Nicolson Maps
3 Frazer Street, Largs
Tel: 01475 689242

Site categories

Best remote sites: Carradale Bay Caravan Park, Kilvrecht Caravan and Camp Site, Portnadoran Caravan Site, Glenmore Camping and Caravanning Site, Cannich Caravan and Camping Site, Sands Caravan and Camping Park, Horgabost Campsite, Clachtoll Beach Campsite, Skeld Caravan and Camping Site

Best island sites: Shieling Holidays, Horgabost Campsite, Pickaquoy Centre Caravan and Camping Park, Skeld Caravan and Camping Site

Best sites close to a town or village: Kippford Holiday Park, Carradale Bay Caravan Park, Woodlands Caravan Park, Lochside Caravan Club Site, Blair Castle Caravan Park, Ballater Caravan Park, Haughton Caravan Park, Grantown on Spey Caravan Park, Cannich Caravan and Camping Site, Banff Links Caravan Park, Pickaquoy Centre Caravan and Camping Park

Best sites close to wild camping: Comrie Croft Eco Camping, Kilvrecht Caravan and Camp Site, Horgabost Campsite

Best countryside park sites: Hoddom Castle Caravan Park, Beecraigs Caravan and Camping Site, Blair Castle Caravan Park, Haughton Caravan Park, Aden Caravan Park

Best sites with leisure/sports facilities: Lochside Caravan Club Site, Pickaquoy Centre Caravan and Camping Park

Best holiday park sites: Kippford Holiday Park, Deeside Holiday Park

Best lochside sites: Lochside Caravan Club Site, Kilvrecht Caravan and Camp Site, Glenmore Camping and Caravanning Site

Best seaside sites: Carradale Bay Caravan Park, Yellowcraig Caravan Club Site, Shieling Holidays, Woodlands Caravan Park, Portnadoran Caravan Site, Banff Links Caravan Park, Sands Caravan and Camping Park, Horgabost Campsite, Clachtoll Beach Campsite, Skeld Caravan and Camping Site

Best National Park sites: Loch Lomond and the Trossachs National Park: Cobleland Caravan and Camping Site; Cairngorm National Park: Invernahavon Caravan Site, Ballater Caravan Park, Glenmore Camping and Caravanning Site, Grantown on Spey Caravan Park

Best new sites: Nydie Caravan and Camping Site, Noah's Ark Caravan Park, Horgabost Campsite, Skeld Caravan and Camping Site

Best sites for public transport: Blair Castle Caravan Park, Portnadoran Caravan Site, Haughton Caravan Park, Deeside Holiday Park, Noah's Ark Caravan Park, Shieling Holidays

Best Caravan Club sites open to non-members: Yellowcraig Caravan Club Site, Lochside Caravan Club Site

Best caravan- and motorhome-only sites: Yellowcraig Caravan Club Site

Kippford Holiday Park

Kippford
Near Dalbeattie
Kirkcudbrightshire
DG5 4LF
Tel: 01556 620636
Website: www.scottishcamping.com/
kippford
Email: info@kippfordholidaypark.co.uk

Kippford Holiday Park is situated in an elevated position offering outstanding views of the Galloway Hills. The lovely waterside village of Kippford is only a 10-minute walk away and is reached by a roadside pavement which passes farmland fields with animals. Kippford has a small picturesque harbour, shop and child-friendly hotels and from here it is possible to walk the 2km Jubilee path to Rockcliffe passing the Mote of Mark hill fort on the way.

The park is well laid out and properly maintained. Tent campers are offered uniquely flat, landscaped pitches which give a feeling of seclusion from neighbours. The touring pitches for motorhomes and caravans have also been levelled and are set out in small groups, and most pitches also have their own electric hookups. The main attractions for families are the well-maintained onsite facilities. For younger visitors there is a central play area, while for older children there is a separate activity area with a flying fox, climbing frame and outdoor shelter.

The local area also offers a diversity of activities and child-centred experiences that should add to your holiday. From one end of the site you can access the local Craigieknowes nine-hole golf course, ideal for beginners and with its own café, while just across the road from the entrance you can gain access to the paths and trails in Dalbeattie Forest, home to one of the 7 stanes mountain biking trails.

The site has its own lovely woodland walks and wildlife and younger visitors will

One of the best!

enjoy the experience of being able to get up close to the park's wildlife, which includes the resident red squirrel population and tame rabbits. Further afield from the site it is easy to access great beaches by car.

Reviews

One of the best!

I have been to lots of camping and caravan sites in Scotland and this is one of the best. Very clean, quiet and well looked after. Tent pitches are all level and the park seems to have been specially landscaped to accommodate tents. Good facilities for kids and lots to do locally. I will go back again. One tip, though, book in advance or you may be disappointed.
Comment by Paul from Shotts

One of the best we've stayed at. Loos and showers spotlessly clean. Pitches carefully arranged, site team incredibly helpful at getting three families pitched near to each other. Will definitely be back – one of our favourite sites.
Comment by Team Roly Mo from York
Type of accommodation: Camper

We were mountain biking at the 7stanes and found it really handy for this. The way the pitches are set out gives it a private feel and there are wild rabbits and red squirrels about which is a nice change for a city dweller!
Comment by Beth & Steven
from Edinburgh
Type of accommodation: Tent

- **TOTAL PITCHES:** 160
- **OPEN FROM:** all year round. Booking is recommended during peak times and especially during July and August.
- **UNITS ACCEPTED:** tents, motorhomes and touring caravans. Wooden cabins and static caravans are available to rent.
- **FACILITIES:** onsite shop open most of the year; disabled-friendly facility block with toilets and free showers; fully equipped laundry; most pitches have access to electric hookups and 'super pitches' also available with water and waste connections; chemical disposal point; telephone; pets welcome
- **CHILD-SPECIFIC FACILITIES:** baby changing; heated facility block; games room; cooking shelter/campers' kitchen; wildlife onsite; local nature trails; play park
- **LOCAL CHILD-FRIENDLY ATTRACTIONS (FREE):** local beaches and nature trails; 7 stanes mountain biking for older children
- **LOCAL CHILD-FRIENDLY ATTRACTIONS (WITH A CHARGE):** Mabie Farm Park within 10 miles; Cream O'Galloway visitors' centre with indoor and outdoor children's adventure; pony trekking
- **POOR-WEATHER ACTIVITIES:** Dumfries offers the DG One swimming pool and leisure centre
- **NEAREST CHILD-FRIENDLY BAR/RESTAURANT:** two local child-friendly restaurants/bars in Kippford village

Beeswing Caravan Park

Kirkgunzeon
Dumfries
DG2 8JL
Tel: 01387 760242
Website: www.scottishcamping.com/
beeswing
Email: beeswingcaravan@aol.com

Beeswing is a small, family-run site nestling in Galloway countryside. Set in 15 acres of landscaped grounds of trees, shrubs and wildlife areas, Beeswing provides an ideal natural playground for younger children. Families love this site and the reviews prove it!

Large, spaced pitches provide freedom for kids to run and play in safety. The site also offers a play area with swings, a sandpit and kick-about area and a putting green. Away from the camping area is an 8-acre field with newly planted woodland, a stream, ponds and a small river. It provides an ideal place to introduce children to natural spaces, birds and wildlife. They can also meet Benjamin the donkey and the 'free range' chickens. Even though the stream and ponds onsite are some distance from the camping area and are fenced or gated off, parents should still ensure all children are appropriately supervised. The shallow stream is suitable for dam building and pond dipping.

The site is well maintained and offers grass pitches (24 in total, most of which have electrics); with no streetlights onsite this allows campers an under-the-stars experience.

This is an ideal site for families with younger children, given the range of facilities. It also provides a central base for exploring the local area and numerous visitor attractions (including 7 stanes) which are only a short car journey away on quiet roads. Late arrivals are not encouraged to ensure that campers with children are not disturbed late at night.

Our kids loved the playpark and wildlife

Reviews

Had the pleasure of staying at Beeswing for three nights last week and it was one of the loveliest spots we have had the good fortune to come across. The site is lovely and the kids' play area is great, as is the small putting area. Benjamin the donkey is also another highlight for the kids. The surroundings are beautiful, especially the ponds and the wildlife they attract. Would highly recommend it to anyone, especially families with young children. One of the nicest and friendliest sites we have visited.
Comment by Taylor Family from Leslie, Fife
Type of accommodation: Tent

Fantastic site, in a lovely peaceful rural setting with spotless facilities throughout – one of the best sites we've ever stayed at. It was also relatively quiet considering it was mid July. The owners are very friendly and charge very little in comparison to other sites – excellent value for money. Our kids loved the playpark and wildlife around the onsite ponds. Its location is ideal for visiting family attractions such as Cream o'Galloway and Mabie Farm Park. We'll definitely return in the near future.
Comment by Ian & Sandra from Edinburgh
Type of accommodation: Tent

- **TOTAL PITCHES:** 24
- **OPEN FROM:** 1 March to 31 October. Advanced booking is always recommended and essential during peak periods.
- **UNITS ACCEPTED:** tents, motorhomes and touring caravans. Static caravans are available to rent.
- **FACILITIES:** disabled-friendly facility block with free showers; electric hookups; laundry facilities including washing machine, tumble dryer, drying area and clothes line; pets welcome
- **CHILD-SPECIFIC FACILITIES:** baby changing; baby/toddlers' bath available; separate room with shower and toilet suitable for younger children; heated facility block; farm animals onsite; local nature trails; play park
- **LOCAL CHILD-FRIENDLY ATTRACTIONS (FREE):** Dumfries: Camera Obscura and Museum and Gracefield Arts Centre; small museum at Dalbeattie; Galloway Kite Trail; 7 stanes mountain-bike trails; Cycling routes: Kirkpatrick McMillan Trail, Fantastic forest (Dalbeattie and Mabie – all abilities); Drumcoltran Tower (a short walk from the caravan park); Coastal walk to Kippford; Galloway Forest Park: Queens Way and Deer Park
- **LOCAL CHILD-FRIENDLY ATTRACTIONS (WITH A CHARGE):** Dumfries: DG One swimming pool and leisure complex; RSPB reserves at Mersehead and Loch Ken; near Dumfries: Caerlaverock Castle and Wildfowl and Wetlands Trust; Cream o' Galloway near Gatehouse of Fleet: ice cream and excellent adventure playground; Loch Ken and Kippford: sailing and other water sports; Leadhills Railway (volunteer-run and great fun)
- **POOR-WEATHER ACTIVITIES:** Dumfries: Farmers Den and Dalscone Farm (indoor play areas); Mabie Farm Park near Dumfries (with indoor play area); Drumlanrig Castle and Country Park: excellent adventure playground; Dalton Pottery: make and paint your own pottery; Twynholm: chocolate factory; New Abbey: museum of costume (Shambellie House), working corn mill and Sweetheart Abbey

Hoddom Castle Caravan Park

Hoddom
Lockerbie
Dumfriesshire
DG11 1AS
Tel: 01576 300251
Website: www.scottishcamping.com/
hoddom
Email: enquiries@hoddomcastle.co.uk

Hoddom Castle Caravan Park is located near Lockerbie close to the Scottish border. It is an ideal site for those heading north into Scotland or looking for a break away from the central belt of Scotland, as it is just a two-hour drive from Glasgow and Edinburgh. The site is conveniently located just minutes from the main M74 motorway.

The site is set in partially wooded parkland in the grounds of a sixteenth-century border keep forming part of the 10,000-acre Hoddom and Kinmount Estates. The River Annan and Hoddom Castle Golf Course bound the site to the north and east – and these areas provide just some of the many activities available at the site. Given that the river could pose a potential hazard, adults are asked to appropriately supervise children onsite.

The site is the perfect base for exploring Dumfriesshire and the south of Scotland but, like many families, you may decide not to venture far given that there are so many opportunities onsite to keep yourselves entertained. You and the kids are welcome to join the Countryside Ranger on guided walks which could include activities such as checking bird boxes, badger watching, spotting wild deer, building bridges, planting trees or carrying out surveys on the beach. You could alternatively make time for the visitors' centre or playground, or try some of the other activities available for kids onsite, including tennis, golf, fishing and mountain-biking.

A campsite with its own castle!

The site has modern facilities including a shop, bar and restaurant, all of which offer disabled access. The bar and restaurant are set within two separate rooms both within the castle itself. The restaurant provides a full service for dinner as well as a takeaway service. The shop provides the essentials such as fresh bread, milk and butter and is licensed.

Hoddom really is an ideal family park.

Reviews

What a fantastic camp site. Having been to many sites around Scotland, this is the best by miles. The showers are spotless, we found all the staff very warm and friendly and the setting was stunning – our tent looked over the castle and the kids loved the fact the loos, bar, games room etc are all inside the castle. We will be going back as soon as we can. Fantastic!
Comment by unknown from Glasgow
Type of accommodation: Tent

Great tenting area, tho can get busy during English school hols when large tents can make elec hookup area seem a bit cramped. Huge site with loads of walks/trails for kids and bikes. Even when busy in August, seemed to be plenty of showers/toilets etc to go round. Shop onsite will bail you out for basics, but Annan only 5 mins away with everything you need. Loads to do in this area if you have active kids: quads, go-karts, paintball etc, and you should try out the dirt buggies at 'Farm buggy trails', great fun for young and old alike. All in all a great place to stay and would certainly return.
Edited comment by the Lamb Family from Markinch, Fife
Type of accommodation: Tent

- **TOTAL PITCHES:** 65 touring and 40 tent camping
- **OPEN FROM:** 1 April to 31 October. Booking is essential for school holiday periods and bank holidays when there is a minimum three-night stay policy.
- **UNITS ACCEPTED:** tents, motorhomes and touring caravans. Wooden cabins are available to rent.
- **FACILITIES:** onsite shop; disabled-friendly facility block with toilets and showers; laundry; pets welcome
- **CHILD-SPECIFIC FACILITIES:** baby changing; heated facility block; games room; local nature trails; play park
- **LOCAL CHILD-FRIENDLY ATTRACTIONS (FREE):** nature trails; mountain-biking track onsite; tennis courts; ranger activities
- **LOCAL CHILD-FRIENDLY ATTRACTIONS (WITH A CHARGE):** DG One swimming and leisure centre in Dumfries; swimming in Annan; Mabie Farm Park; Cream O'Galloway visitors' centre with indoor and outdoor children's adventure; horse riding at Powfoot and Brydekirk
- **POOR-WEATHER ACTIVITIES:** Several indoor play centres in Dumfries and Galloway area
- **NEAREST CHILD-FRIENDLY BAR/RESTAURANT:** Onsite

Carradale Bay Caravan Park

Carradale
Kintyre
Argyll
PA28 6QG
Tel: 01583 431665
Website: www.scottishcamping.com/
carradale
Email: info@carradalebay.com

Situated on the edge of Carradale Bay, one of the best beaches on the Kintyre peninsula, this spacious site boasts panoramic views over the sea and surrounding countryside, with the Isle of Arran offering a glorious backdrop in one direction and wooded hills in the other. This is an ideal location for island-hopping from this Kintyre base.

If you are looking for a holiday with something for all the family to do, as individuals or together, try Carradale. The more active visitor can enjoy safe bathing and water sports from the large sandy beach. There is also the opportunity to go walking, cycling, pony trekking and fishing both sea and game. For golfing enthusiasts there is the Carradale golf course and the world-famous championship course at Machrihanish further afield.

The village of Carradale is an appealing short walk or cycle away and has shops, bars and restaurants. There are several coastal and forest trails which can be undertaken from the site and which may easily include a refreshment stop in the village. On a good day the waymarked walk up to the top of the local Cnoc Nan Gabhar hill (230m) is a favourite and the summit offers fine views over the Kilbrannan Sound to the jagged northern peaks of Arran.

The site itself is laid out in small grass bays offering shelter and the feeling of being on a much smaller site, with a very relaxed atmosphere. As a consequence the site has received many awards, including Winner of the Best Caravan and Camping Park Tourism Award, plus an AA award for Attractive Environment five years running.

One of the most beautiful locations imaginable

This park is situated in an area of outstanding natural beauty. It has a lovely feeling of seclusion. Set in a southerly corner of the Carradale Estate, it has easy access to the extensive Carradale Bay with over a mile of golden sands.

The site is affiliated to the Caravan Club.

Reviews

Must be in one of the loveliest spots in Scotland (and we've tried most ...). The beach is only yards away and stunning views whichever direction you look. The site itself is mainly grass but pitches are firm enough and far enough away from your neighbour's. Great walks all over the area and two or three pubs within a good walking distance. Facilities are starting to look a little weary but in spite of that I'd be back tomorrow if I could! The journey there is also very scenic and on a good day you can't beat it. Also good for dogs as there is a river nearby too for canine water lovers.
Comment by Jan from Lancashire
Type of accommodation: Camper

Great site – very nice owners, right next to beach. Great bakery in Carradale. Nice toilet blocks. There wasn't actually a play park onsite but there was loads of space to play, site nicely laid out and there is a beach right next to it and a nice 9-hole golf course nearby and a small mountain bike track for kids in Carradale so loads to do.
Comment by J Wilson from Glasgow

Superb coastal scenery backed by hilly lush mixed woodland. The area is served by well signposted walks. The site itself is well laid out with bushes and shrubs creating about 5 or 6 areas each of around a dozen well spaced level pitches. The long beach is very gently sloping and child-safe. Rabbits grazing and snoozing round the vans kept us entertained. Nothing on-site for kids but there are acres and acres of safe beach, low dunes, grassland and woods to explore. Staff are absolute gems!
Comment by Dave W from Near Perth

- **TOTAL PITCHES:** 60
- **OPEN FROM:** Easter to 30 September
- **UNITS ACCEPTED:** tents, motorhomes and touring caravans. Wooden wigwams and static caravans are available to rent.
- **FACILITIES:** toilet and shower blocks providing ample facilities; electric hookups; Elsan disposal for the emptying of chemical toilets; laundry; open campfires allowed on beach only; pets accepted
- **CHILD-SPECIFIC FACILITIES:** cooking shelter/campers' kitchen; wildlife onsite; local nature trails
- **LOCAL CHILD-FRIENDLY ATTRACTIONS (FREE):** great beach on your doorstep to explore; National Cycle Network route 78: Oban to Campbeltown; Mull of Kintyre; Isle of Arran, Islay and Jura; Saddell Abbey; Owl Centre; forest walks
- **LOCAL CHILD-FRIENDLY ATTRACTIONS (WITH A CHARGE):** water sports within 8km
- **POOR-WEATHER ACTIVITIES:** Saddell Abbey; Owl Centre
- **NEAREST CHILD-FRIENDLY BAR/RESTAURANT:** Several local family-friendly restaurants and bars within the village

Beecraigs Caravan and Camping Site

Beecraigs Country Park
Linlithgow
West Lothian
EH49 6PL
Tel: 01506 844516
Website: www.scottishcamping.com/
beecraigs
Email: mail@beecraigs.com

Beecraigs Caravan and Camping Site is situated only 5km from the historic town of Linlithgow and within the Bathgate Hills. It offers free access to the extensive country park which has a wide range of onsite activities and potential adventures to keep all children entertained. The site can be easily accessed by car from much of the central belt of Scotland and offers a peaceful escape for a weekend or longer. Linlithgow train station is 5km away.

An extremely spacious 1,000-acre country park surrounds the camping area and this includes a deer park, restaurant, sawmill and fishery stocked with rainbow trout. There is an onsite ranger service and outdoor centre offering many activities and walks. It also boasts a Go Ape high-wire forest adventure for kids.

If you intend to visit Linlithgow you will discover a historic town that is home to the magnificent ruined Linlithgow Palace, located in the town centre. Behind the palace you will find the Peel, with its loch and parklands. These are great for exploring and discovering wildlife; you can walk right round the Peel in about an hour.

The camping and caravan site itself offers visitors hardstanding pitches for motorhomes and touring caravans. There are five designated tourers' areas each of which can accommodate up to six vans. These are serviced by electric hookups, water stands and waste points. Tents are accommodated on grass pitches within the lower landscaped camping area, while there is a further upper campsite also available for private group hire. There are no electric hookups for tent campers. The site has two

Great site, plenty for the kids to do

conveniently located facility blocks. There is no charge for children under five years of age and dogs on the site. There is no shop onsite or within the country park.

Reviews

Very peaceful, hardstanding pitches for caravans make it ideal for winter caravanning. The caravan layout is lovely – lots of little 'pods' for 5 or 6 units to pitch, each with water and waste area and each pitch separated by planting of various kinds. Lots of tall trees surround the site. The site is set in the Beecraigs Country Park near Linlithgow – loads of shops and the fascinating ruined palace – birthplace of Mary, Queen of Scots. It's only about half an hour to Edinburgh but the site has the pleasantness of being in the country. In the park are masses of things to do – cycling or walking everywhere, a fish farm, loch, forest to explore and a fantastic children's play area – huge and set up in age-specific areas. There are also numerous wee play parks around the site The bathrooms are spectacular. Each shower is in its own wee room with loo, sink and mirror. They were wonderfully warm in Feb – fan heater in each shower room and in the corridor. Also they were immaculate! I would thoroughly recommend this site. I will be back asap!
Comment by Elaine from Dollar
Type of accommodation: Caravan

Visited last week for the first time, great site, plenty for the kids to do. Toilets immaculate. Most of the trees have been cut down surrounding the site so it is now delightfully spacious and sunny (sometimes). Would not hesitate to recommend to anyone. Will be returning as soon as possible.
Comment by Ken Reid
from Cumbernauld
Type of accommodation: Camper

Lovely site with excellent facilities, washrooms amazing! Great area for walks, wildlife. All pitches separated by low hedges, so good for privacy. Will certainly be back.
Comment by Kate from Scotland
Type of accommodation: Camper

- ■ **TOTAL PITCHES:** 36
- ■ **OPEN FROM:** all year round. Advance booking is strongly recommended at all times.
- ■ **UNITS ACCEPTED:** tents, motorhomes and touring caravans
- ■ **FACILITIES:** two facility blocks with toilets and showers; disabled washroom; electric hookups; shaving points; hand and hair dryers; launderette; dishwashing room; public telephone; barbecues and Calor Gas exchange
- ■ **CHILD-SPECIFIC FACILITIES:** baby changing; heated toilet block; family rooms with showers; children's bath; small onsite play area
- ■ **LOCAL CHILD-FRIENDLY ATTRACTIONS (FREE):** access to the country park, fishing for juniors is offered free with full paying adult; walks and nature trails; onsite wildlife
- ■ **LOCAL CHILD-FRIENDLY ATTRACTIONS (WITH A CHARGE):** Beecraigs Go Ape high-wire forest adventure course; sports centre in Linlithgow; Linlithgow Palace and Peel; Almond Valley heritage centre
- ■ **POOR-WEATHER ACTIVITIES:** easy to visit Edinburgh, Glasgow and other central belt attractions
- ■ **NEAREST CHILD-FRIENDLY BAR/RESTAURANT:** child-friendly restaurants within park and nearest bar 5km

Yellowcraig Caravan Club Site

Dirleton
East Lothian
EH39 5DS
Tel: 01620 850217
Website: www.scottishcamping.com/
yellowcraig

Yellowcraig Caravan Club Site is located on the East Lothian coast close to Dirleton, a small historic village between the towns of Gullane and North Berwick.

Dirleton Village is home to Dirleton Castle, which has stood for over 400 years as a fortress. There is a small local shop and two hotels. North Berwick, 5km from the site, is a town offering a full range of shops and services. It is home to the Millennium Commission-funded Scottish Seabird Centre, which uses remote-controlled cameras to view Scotland's seabirds, as well as a spectacular Gannet Experience sound and light show. North Berwick's location affords exceptional views of the Bass Rock and other islands and offers boat trips from the harbour to view the wildlife.

The site itself is located less than 2km from the village, next to Yellowcraig beach with its surrounding dune system and woodland areas. These are a fantastic natural resource and have been a magnet to families for generations. It is a very attractive site and offers several pitching areas separated by grassy banks, shrubs and rose bushes. It is a splendid choice for family holidays, being as well run and organised as you would expect from a Caravan Club site. Non-members of the club are, however, expected to either join the Club or pay a supplement.

 A short walk of less than 500m from the site entrance will bring you to the wonderful Yellowcraigs Broad Sands beach which has acres of magnificent golden sands and offers great views out to Fidra Island and its lighthouse. Before you reach the beach

A wonderful play area and the gorgeous beach make it a good place for kids

there is also an extensive woodland play area with nature trails for children. Nature lovers will enjoy the birds and wildlife that abound in the woodlands and dunes. The area is also large enough that even at busy times everyone is able to find their own nooks and crannies.

Reviews

We have stayed here three times and enjoyed it every time, the wildlife is everywhere so beware of the rabbit holes, excellent location as you are next to a big CLEAN beach and a woodland, so great for kids and dogs alike. Also there is an adventure play area in the woods: you will walk past this en route to the beach. Close to villages and easy access to Edinburgh and the Borders, again excellent Caravan Club facilities.
Edited comment by Davie H from Fife
Type of accommodation: Caravan

A site we frequently use for stop-offs on our way on or returning from holiday. Can be very busy (on a number of occasions we have stayed there the site has been full) but is nicely divided up into distinct areas so doesn't feel overcrowded. Close proximity of a wonderful play area and the gorgeous beach make it a good place for kids.
Comment by Team Roly Mo from York
Type of accommodation: Camper

Wonderful location, clean showers and loos and a child-friendly site. Even though it was busy with bikes and kids everywhere, it never felt overcrowded or noisy due to banked areas. Lovely beach nearby with adventure playground in woods. Very windy though!
Comment by MJRK from Perthshire
Type of accommodation: Caravan

- **TOTAL PITCHES:** 116
- **OPEN FROM:** end March to early November
- **UNITS ACCEPTED:** motorhomes and touring caravans only; NO TENTS
- **FACILITIES:** Toilet and shower blocks providing ample facilities; disabled facilities; electric hookups; Elsan disposal for the emptying of chemical toilets; laundry; pets accepted
- **CHILD-SPECIFIC FACILITIES:** baby changing; play park
- **LOCAL CHILD-FRIENDLY ATTRACTIONS (FREE):** sea fishing from beach and rocks; adventure park close by; great beach and dunes to explore
- **LOCAL CHILD-FRIENDLY ATTRACTIONS (WITH A CHARGE):** sports activities including water-skiing, sailing, windsurfing and 19 golf courses; Scottish Mining Museum; East Fortune Museum of Flight; Dirleton Castle ruins; Lennoxlove House; the Royal Yacht Britannia; the Scottish Sea Bird Centre; East Links Farm, Dunbar
- **POOR-WEATHER ACTIVITIES:** Scottish Mining Museum; East Fortune Museum of Flight; Lennoxlove House; Dunbar Leisure Pool
- **NEAREST CHILD-FRIENDLY BAR/RESTAURANT:** Three local child-friendly restaurants and bars within 5km

Cobleland Caravan and Camping Site

Forest Holidays
Station Road
Gartmore
Stirlingshire
FK8 3RR
Tel: (bookings) 0845 130 8224; (site)
01877 382392
Website: www.scottishcamping.com/
cobleland
Email: info@forestholidays.co.uk

Cobleland sits on the banks of the River Forth, shaded by majestic old oak trees. It is set within the Queen Elizabeth Forest Park which is part of Loch Lomond and the Trossachs National Park. The site is conveniently located close to the village of Aberfoyle (2km), which has a supermarket and several places to eat.

There is a vast number of activities for young and old alike, including a choice of stunning walking or cycling trails, as well as opportunities for fishing or picnicking. The Queen Elizabeth Forest Park is also home to the Go Ape high-wire adventure course, which boasts the longest zip wire in Britain. The site is also on the national cycling network (route 7), which provides a direct path to Aberfoyle (a 30-minute walk).

For those interested in the geological history of this wild landscape, a walk on the Highland Boundary Fault Trail from the park's visitor centre is not to be missed and given its location the site attracts a wide range of wildlife. This includes native red squirrels, the very elusive Scottish wildcat and a variety of other creatures.

The site is fairly small and is well laid-out. Now that Forest Holidays has teamed up with Eurocamp it also offers pre-pitched tents along with space for the usual units. It has a lovely riverside location but campers with kids should be aware that the River Forth runs down one site of the campsite. When not in spate the river does not pose a hazard to children as long as they are adequately supervised.

The site is located just off the A81 around 2km south of Aberfoyle.

Booked for two nights — stayed seven

Reviews

Recently returned from lovely weekend at Cobleland despite the weather. Well run and friendly. Clean toilets and shower rooms. Well-stocked shop. Plenty freedom and friends for kids. Will certainly be back. Surprise of the trip, no midges!
Comment by the Stefanovic family from Glasgow
Type of accommodation: Tent

This is a great wee site right in the heart of Scotland. Staff are excellent and not o.t.t. as other reviews suggest. This site is run just the way my family and I like it. Enjoy the company of others but also let others have their space. Forests all around so plenty of walking if you wish, a half hour's walk and you are in Aberfoyle town, with some shops and pubs if you wish. All in all a great place to visit for a night or longer. We stayed five nights but wished it could be longer. Will return.
Comment by Tommy from Glasgow
Type of accommodation: Tent

Initially booked for two nights but enjoyed Cobleland so much we stayed seven nights! Wardens Graeme and Lesley gave us a friendly welcome and were extremely helpful and pleasant throughout our stay. Toilets and showers were kept clean and tidy. The site, situated on the River Forth, is ideally located for many scenic drives and forest walks. It is worth visiting the David Marshall visitor centre above Aberfoyle (a few minutes' drive from the site) as a good introduction to the area. We hope we can return soon!
Comment by Lochnessmonster from beside Loch Ness of course!!
Type of accommodation: Caravan

- **TOTAL PITCHES:** 126
- **OPEN FROM:** 25 March to 31 October
- **UNITS ACCEPTED:** tents, motorhomes, touring caravans and new pre-pitched tents
- **FACILITIES:** Heated toilet and shower blocks providing ample facilities; disabled facilities; electric hookups; onsite shop; chemical disposal point; showers; laundry; pets accepted
- **CHILD-SPECIFIC FACILITIES:** heated toilet block; wildlife onsite; local nature trails; children's play area
- **LOCAL CHILD-FRIENDLY ATTRACTIONS (FREE):** onsite treasure hunts and scavenger hunts; ranger activities; picnic area with paddling in the river and free fishing; offsite David Marshall Lodge has free swing park, squirrel hide and some free ranger activities; local park in Aberfoyle; Village Wool Mill in Aberfoyle also holds free events
- **LOCAL CHILD-FRIENDLY ATTRACTIONS (WITH A CHARGE):** Rednock Pony Trekking; Hamilton Toy Museum, Callander
- **POOR-WEATHER ACTIVITIES:** David Marshall Lodge; swimming at Callander; Stirling Castle and Wallace Monument, Stirling
- **NEAREST CHILD-FRIENDLY BAR/RESTAURANT:** there are three to choose from: the Coach House Pub and the Forth Inn, both in Aberfoyle (2km) and the Black Bull, Gartmore (2km)

Nydie Caravan and Camping Site

Knockhill of Nydie
Strathkinness
St Andrews
KY16 9SL
Tel: 01334 850110
Website: www.scottishcamping.com/
nydie
Email: enquiry@nydie.co.uk

Nydie Caravan and Camping Site is a new kid on the camping block, having only opened in 2008, but it is already established as a favourite.

The 10-acre site is approximately 5km from St Andrews and offers a family-focused camping experience in Fife. It is just a short walk into the village of Strathkinness, where The Tavern serves food seven days a week and there is a shop, a post office and two well-equipped play parks.

At the campsite you and your family are sure to receive a warm welcome as Sue and Sam, the site owners, have made their site totally accessible and safe for families, from the play area that can be seen from all areas of the site to the baby changing and family shower rooms. They understand that children like to play and as a result have catered for this with a mini football pitch, play park and various games to borrow such as giant jenga, a cricket set and a multipurpose sports net. They have also established onsite a small shop that sells the award-winning Jannetta's ice cream from St Andrews.

From Nydie Caravan and Camping Site there are stunning views over St Andrews bay. This is an ideal base for exploring the quaint fishing villages of the East Neuk and St Andrews itself. The surrounding areas are not all about golf and local attractions for the children include the beautiful beaches and nature reserves.

Brilliant fun!

Reviews

- **TOTAL PITCHES:** 35
- **OPEN FROM:** April to September
- **UNITS ACCEPTED:** tents, motorhomes, touring caravans and wooden wigwams
- **FACILITIES:** toilet and shower block; disabled facilities; separate dishwashing area; shop; camp kitchen; chemical disposal; open campfires allowed; pet-friendly
- **CHILD-SPECIFIC FACILITIES:** baby changing; heated facility block; local nature trails; play park and play area for ball games
- **LOCAL CHILD-FRIENDLY ATTRACTIONS (FREE):** Allan Hill fruit farm and play area; Strathkinness parks (2); St Andrews beaches; Tentsmuir forest beach and walks; Eden Estuary nature reserve; coastal paths
- **LOCAL CHILD-FRIENDLY ATTRACTIONS (WITH A CHARGE):** St Andrews Aquarium; St Andrews Castle and Cathedral; Craigtoun Country Park adventure park in St Andrews; Cairnie fruit farm and maze; Barbara Field stables; botanic gardens; Kinburn Park; Himalayas putting; Scotland's secret bunker; Isle of May boat trips
- **POOR-WEATHER ACTIVITIES:** East Sands Leisure Pool; St Andrews Aquarium; Deep Sea World; Byre Theatre; Cinema. In nearby Dundee: Discovery Quay and Dundee Leisure Pool
- **NEAREST CHILD-FRIENDLY BAR/RESTAURANT:** The Tavern in Strathkinness, 1.5km from site

Noah's Ark Caravan Park

Newhouse Farm
Western Edge
Perth
PH1 1QF
Tel: 01738 580661
Website: www.scottishcamping.com/
noahsark
Email: info@ noahsarkcaravanpark.co.uk

Noah's Ark Caravan Park opened in 2009 and has already established itself as a family favourite. The caravan park is a recent development complementing the Noah's Ark play centre.

The site is situated on the western edge of Perth, the gateway to the Highlands, and is the perfect place to base your Scottish holiday. The site can easily be accessed from the A9 when heading northwards round the city. It is also on a Perth City bus route.

The site is just over 3km from the city centre which offers a variety of shops, cafés, hotels and child-friendly activities. The town has two large parks on either side of the city, the North Inch and the South Inch, and a modern leisure and swimming centre. Near Perth there are also many castles and historic sites and excellent fishing and golfing.

The Caravan Park with its play centre specialises in fun activities for all the family. In 2011 the site added a new activity centre with both junior and adult quad biking, a climbing wall and bungee trampolines. This development is in addition to the established children's play barn with go-karts, bowling, ceramics and a restaurant. With the golf driving range and crazy golf also onsite there really is no reason why families will wish to leave.

Onsite there is a selection of grass and hardstanding pitches for tourers and tents. The site also offers wooden microlodges and octolodges which are great fun if you enjoy camping but fancy a bit more luxury.

Great new site!

Reviews

1st class site ideal for kids, lots to do, mini golf, go-karting, ten pin bowling and soft play, great value for money!!! Great central location too.
Comment by Stu V from Stirling
Type of accommodation: Tent

Had a great weekend, with wife and 2 young children. Lovely small campsite. Staff were very friendly, putting in additional swings on the morning we arrived that were in full use by lunch time. Lots to do for children. Toilets small but very clean. We will certainly be back.
Comment by Gary Smith from Glasgow.
Type of accommodation: Caravan

Just spent six enjoyable days at this site, wardens very helpful and made us most welcome when we arrived, the site was very clean and tidy, spacious showers and a very good washing up area and laundry, very good bus service just 5 minutes' walk from the site every 10 minutes takes you into the centre of Perth. The views are also great, will certainly be back soon.
Comment by Margaret McGillivray from Ellon
Type of accommodation: Caravan

Great new site. Lots of lovely walks in area with bus stop just along the road with regular buses taking you straight into Perth city centre. Large pitches. Looking forward to larger washing/showering facilities in future. Will also def. bring the grandchildren.
Comment by Robertson from Brechin
Type of accommodation: Camper

- **TOTAL PITCHES:** 40
- **OPEN FROM:** March to November
- **UNITS ACCEPTED:** tents, motorhomes, touring caravans. Wooden microlodges (sleep 4) and octolodges (sleep 6) available onsite.
- **FACILITIES:** modern heated toilet and shower block; disabled facilities; laundry; electric hookups; pet-friendly
- **CHILD-SPECIFIC FACILITIES:** baby-changing; heated facility block; local nature trails; play park
- **LOCAL CHILD-FRIENDLY ATTRACTIONS (FREE):** the North and South Inch parks in Perth, with play parks and child-friendly facilities
- **LOCAL CHILD-FRIENDLY ATTRACTIONS (WITH A CHARGE):** outdoor and indoor activity centres onsite; swimming pool 4km
- **POOR-WEATHER ACTIVITIES:** local castles and palaces; Perth swimming pool and onsite play barn
- **NEAREST CHILD-FRIENDLY BAR/RESTAURANT:** restaurant onsite and several child-friendly hotels within 4km

Comrie Croft Eco Camping

Braincroft
Crieff
Perthshire
PH7 4JZ
Tel: 01764 670140
Website: www.scottishcamping.com/
comriecroft
Email: info@comriecroft.com

Comrie Croft offers a wild camping experience without the hardship – including plenty of hot showers and toilets. The croft campsite is located at the foot of the southern slopes of the local munro Ben Chonzie which is on the southern edge of the Highlands. The site occupies a farmstead conversion just over an hour's drive from Edinburgh or Glasgow. This area of Perthshire has a great deal to offer families, even when it rains, and the site's family-friendly pricing policy of allowing under 5s to camp free and under 16s for half price should make a camping trip here easier on your pocket.

The employee-owned Comrie Croft site offers a variety of habitats in which to pitch your tent, including secluded pitches among the open birchwood, elevated meadow or a picturesque pitch in a sunny field offering stunning views out towards the surrounding hills. Fire pits (wood is for sale or bring your own) for campers and hammocks are provided.

Families if they wish an alternative to their own tent can choose to hire one of the site's unique Swedish kata tents, complete with woodburning stoves, hand-made bed and furniture, sheepskin rugs and oil lamps.

Onsite there is bike hire, walking trails, a shop, an indoor games room and barn and baby-changing facilities. In 2011 an informal children's adventure play area was created in the woods along with 'La Tienda' – a tea/coffee/snacks shed with access to hot water and a microwave.

Wild camping with a difference!

Comrie Croft is located well away from the main road, allowing parents to relax while their children let off steam and explore a 'safe' woodland environment. There are several natural hazards, including a stream, steep ground and a pond, as you would expect in such a natural setting. More creative kids will have opportunities to guddle in the burn and make dens in the woods.

Reviews

What a marvellous place. The wardens and staff were more helpful and friendly than some 5 star hotels I have been to. Great location and close enough to lots of other places of interest although my 5 year old daughter was more than happy to play in the games barn and go on forest walks. Discovering a pond full of maturing tadpoles and suitable for swimming in was a real treasure. The opportunity to have campfires is a treat indeed. Showers and toilets were very clean and well maintained and it was good to see that the site has thought about accessibility for disabled campers, eg the washing up sink has been lowered. Site staff had good local knowledge and went to the ends of the earth to get information for us. All in all, a lovely experience and we will definitely be back.
Edited comment by Lindsey and Eva from Scotland
Type of accommodation: Tent

Had a great night here and it's mid September!! The weather stayed nice and bright. We enjoyed the nice walks around the campsite and feeding the birds. The woodland pitch we had was very secluded which suited us fine as we were there to chill out, also had great fun building the fire and toasting marshmallows. One of our best camping experiences this summer and we've had a good few! Would definitely recommend this campsite to all. We can't wait to go back!
Comment by Davie, Lorraine & Louise Cathro from Dundee
Type of accommodation: Tent

- **TOTAL PITCHES:** 24
- **OPEN FROM:** April to October; booking only required during July and August
- **UNITS ACCEPTED:** take your own tent or rent pre-erected Swedish kata tents
- **FACILITIES:** heated toilet and shower block; disabled facilities; baby changing; shop; games room; open campfires allowed; pets accepted
- **CHILD-SPECIFIC FACILITIES:** baby changing; heated toilet block; tea and coffee shed with microwave; wildlife onsite; local nature trails; play park
- **LOCAL CHILD-FRIENDLY ATTRACTIONS (FREE):** waymarked trails leading to monuments and waterfalls; Macrosty Park in Crieff (a very child-friendly attraction offering large play areas and picnic areas); Loch Lomond National Park at Loch Earn is close by
- **LOCAL CHILD-FRIENDLY ATTRACTIONS (WITH A CHARGE):** Auchingarrich Wildlife Centre; Raptor World; Strathearn recreation centre and swimming pool; quad biking, golf etc at Crieff Hydro resort; Crannog Centre at Killin
- **POOR-WEATHER ACTIVITIES:** Auchingarrich Wildlife Centre; Strathearn recreation centre and swimming pool; Famous Grouse Experience and wildlife park; the Ceramic Experience; play your own games in onsite barn
- **NEAREST CHILD-FRIENDLY BAR/RESTAURANT:** the Royal Hotel in Comrie is less than 3km away and can be accessed by a regular bus service

Shieling Holidays

Craignure
Isle of Mull
PA65 6AY
Tel: 01680 812496
Website: www.scottishcamping.com/
shielingholidays or
www.shielingwildlife.co.uk
Email: info@shielingholidays.co.uk

Close to the Craignure ferry terminal connecting the island of Mull to the mainland, Shieling Holidays is an ideal island escape for families. Mull is home not only to Balamory (the BBC children's series modelled on Tobermory, the island's main town) but also to many family-friendly activities and places to visit. From the site you can stroll to the ferry, pub, bistro, steam railway, swimming pool and the bus stops for trips to Iona (for Staffa) and Tobermory (Balamory).

The site offers great views of the mainland and to the distant Ben Nevis. It is situated right on the coast with the sea on two sides and a burn on the other. There is an abundance of wildlife to watch, including the local resident sea otters as well as passing seals and dolphins. The site has its own wildlife website (details above).

From the site entrance visitors to the area, site users, children and well-behaved dogs can enjoy a lovely shoreline walk which runs alongside the steam railway line south towards Torosay Castle. Craignure is both a perfect wildlife haven and a convenient place from which to sample many of the island's best attractions, including castles, beaches, the town of Tobermory and boat trips to Iona and Staffa.

Onsite you are offered well-laid-out pitches for campervans and caravans. Tent campers are accommodated on both organised artificial grass pitches and within a larger camping field. Alongside the traditional camping pitches the site also offers families permanently erected Shieling cottage tents which combine the comfort of a

If Disney made a campsite this would be it!

cottage with the charm of camping and being at one with the environment. For all site users, alongside the usual campsite facilities there is also a common room with a dishwashing area, microwave, TV and multifuel stove.

The site's coastal location offers children numerous opportunities to explore with appropriate supervision and care. Cars are kept out of the main camping field and tents with children are kept away from the onsite crag.

Reviews

If Disney made a campsite this would be it!

Wonderful welcome, and not one blade of grass out of place – and beautifully clean. We are COMPLETE NOVICES but found pitching the tent on astroturf really easy. The views are breathtaking and although we intended to tour we loved the site so much that after two nights' camping we MOVED INTO A SHIELING. Now that's what I call camping – it was fantastic. Own shower and toilet, constant hot water, electricity – I never knew camping could be like this. We are now converted and will definitely be visiting again.
A little piece of heaven.
Comment by the Wards from Newcastle Upon Tyne
Type of accommodation: Tent

Brilliant site with fantastic views from top field. Children well catered for with park, sandpit and swing all close by. Absence of cars onsite makes this site very child-friendly. Free access to common room and tv which was very handy to keep updated with the British Open. Campfire area is a great idea as people given opportunity to socialise overlooking the stunning views and fire helps keep the midges away.
Comment by Carolynne and David from Cumbernauld
Type of accommodation: Tent

- **TOTAL PITCHES:** 30 touring pitches, 60 tent pitches and 15 shielings
- **OPEN FROM:** mid March to end October
- **UNITS ACCEPTED:** tents, motorhomes and touring caravans. Shieling tents are available to rent.
- **FACILITIES:** toilet and shower block with ample facilities; disabled facilities; electric hookups; disposal point for emptying chemical toilets; laundry; games room; pets accepted; open campfire area; wi-fi
- **CHILD-SPECIFIC FACILITIES:** baby-changing; heated toilet block; campers' kitchen/ cooking shelter; wildlife onsite; local nature trails; play park and sandpit
- **LOCAL CHILD-FRIENDLY ATTRACTIONS (FREE):** play park, shingle beach and rock pools onsite; local sandy beaches accessible by car; good walks and nature trails
- **LOCAL CHILD-FRIENDLY ATTRACTIONS (WITH A CHARGE):** swimming pool and gym can be used at Isle of Mull Hotel; boat trips; fishing; pony trekking
- **POOR-WEATHER ACTIVITIES:** swimming pool and gym at Isle of Mull Hotel; Torosay Castle via steam railway from site; Duart Castle (the ancestral home of the Clan Maclean) 5km away; attractions in Tobermory accessible by car or bus
- **NEAREST CHILD-FRIENDLY BAR/RESTAURANT:** Craignure Inn 400m, bistro 800m; Isle of Mull Hotel 2km

Woodlands Caravan Park

Carnoustie
Angus
DD7 6HR
Tel: 01241 854430
Website: www.scottishcamping.com/
woodlands
Email: info@woodlandscaravanpark.net

Woodlands Caravan Park has built itself a big reputation with caravan park and campsite users. Despite it being a small, family-run site, it offers 4.5 acres of flat, well-maintained grassy pitches situated in the grounds of a former mansion house in the burgh of Carnoustie. It is conveniently situated only a ten-minute stroll from Carnoustie town centre which has shops, a post office and child-friendly restaurants and hotels. Carnoustie itself is located just 16km from Dundee.

Carnoustie is famous for its golfing history. The town boasts four courses, including its championship course which last hosted the British Open in 1999. It is also on the main east coast rail line and has a seafront and its own beach, Barry Sands.

Bill and Mary Ferguson recently took over running the site from the local council and are making this a truly superb location for families visiting in caravans, tents and motorhomes. The site facilities are both spacious and clean and there is an onsite recreation room with TV, board games, a pool table and vending machines.

The local leisure centre is a great resource for children when the weather is poor and there is the newly refurbished seafront and popular beach for better days. The park adjacent to the site offers a kids' play area, enough space for family games and room to exercise even the most energetic dog.

You can book by calling the above number or through Carnoustie Leisure Centre on 01241 853246. Contact Bill and Mary Ferguson.

First time camping – so glad we picked this caravan site

Reviews

We do quite a bit of camping and overall this is an excellent site with good-sized flat pitches. The site is quite small with all the facilities very close to the camping area. The wardens were very friendly and had a great sense of humour. The site is very well maintained and the toilet block was spotless, playing piped music 24hrs a day, nice if you have to visit in the middle of the night. My wife was impressed with the ladies as they even had freshly cut flowers in vases. The site is situated next to a large grassland park and children's play area which can be accessed through a secure gate. From the camping area you can see the kids' play area which was quite nice. We stayed for two nights with two kids (2½ yrs and 7 yrs), and my brother-in-law and his son (7 yrs). I would definitely recommend this site for a family visit.
Edited comment by Fifer from Rosyth, Fife
Type of accommodation: Tent

First-time campers with 3 young children, this site is lovely and well run. The shower/toilet block is spotless. There is an indoor room with a pool table and TV which was great for when it rained (which it did!). The park next door has lots to keep kids amused. A 5-minute walk down to the town and the beach – I would recommend this to first-time campers and will definitely return.
Comment by Mrs Forsythe from Stirling
Type of accommodation: Tent

This was my family's first time camping in a tent and I am so glad we picked this caravan site. It was a lovely site. The shower and toilet blocks were clean and well kept. Our two kids enjoyed the play park which was close to the tent. On the last day we went to the beach and found a lovely play park which was only around 10 minutes' walk from the site. There were plenty of places to eat in or take away close by. We will visit again.
Edited comment by Sharon from Fife
Type of accommodation: Tent

- **TOTAL PITCHES:** 40 touring pitches and 15 tent pitches
- **OPEN FROM:** end March until early October
- **UNITS ACCEPTED:** tents, motorhomes and touring caravans
- **FACILITIES:** toilet and shower blocks including disabled facilities; chemical disposal; electric hookups; laundry; games room; pets accepted; wi-fi
- **CHILD-SPECIFIC FACILITIES:** child-friendly heated facilities block onsite which includes baby-changing and disabled shower; dishwashing room with fridge freezer, microwave, toaster, cutlery and crockery
- **LOCAL CHILD-FRIENDLY ATTRACTIONS (FREE):** child-friendly park next to site; beach with newly constructed play area ten minutes' walk away
- **LOCAL CHILD-FRIENDLY ATTRACTIONS (WITH A CHARGE):** swimming pool; leisure centre; fishing; golf courses
- **POOR-WEATHER ACTIVITIES:** Dundee, City of Discovery by local bus outside park or 30 minutes by car; Arbroath by local bus from site or ten minutes by car; more information on local attractions held onsite
- **NEAREST CHILD-FRIENDLY BAR/RESTAURANT:** several local hotels and eateries serve food all day in Carnoustie

Lochside Caravan Club Site

Forfar Country Park
Craig O'Loch Road
Forfar
DD8 1BT
Tel: 01307 468917
Website: www.scottishcamping.com/
lochside

Located next to Forfar Loch on the western side of the town, this site is ideal for active families looking for a town and country break. Forfar is a historic Royal Burgh and the town lies at the heart of the Angus area.

Strongly recommended by families, Lochside Caravan Club Site offers a picturesque parkland location within a few minutes' walk of the bustling centre of Forfar. This award-winning caravan park is situated on the shores of the loch within Forfar Loch Country Park. There is direct access from the site to a 4km walking or cycling trail around the loch which passes woodland, wetland and grasslands that create a haven for wildlife.

The country park also incorporates the Forfar Sailing Club and the Lochside leisure centre. The centre offers access to a variety of outdoor activities, including outdoor tennis courts and football pitches, an 18-hole pitch-and-putt course, an 18-hole putting green and a 9-hole crazy golf course. Inside the centre facilities include a main games hall, a gym, crèche facilities and a café.

The site itself has a central facility block surrounded by 5 acres of flat and grassy parkland incorporating organised pitches for touring caravans, motor caravans and tents.

Forfar is an excellent base from which to explore, and close to the site kids may like to visit Glamis Castle (the childhood home of the Queen Mother), the Angus Glens, which offer spectacular hillwalking, and the rugged cliffs and sandy beaches of the Angus coast.

Queen Mother of sites

Reviews

Queen Mother of sites

1. Clean showers and toilets in heated block with plenty of space to both wash and get dry without getting your clean clothes soaked. 2. Site in the middle of a thriving market town – easy access to shops and pubs. 3. Site right next to a loch and a leisure complex – (no swimming pool) – can go for a walk or run around the loch 2½ miles in total on flat terrain. 4. Angus glens and mountains a few miles away for hill walking. 5.Close to Dundee for shopping, sights etc. Close to Montrose and Brechin – Angus market towns. 6. Fly cup in Forfar at one of the numerous cafés.

Edited comment by Roddy G. from Ellon

This site was ideally located with nice flat pitches, the wardens were more than friendly and helpful, the toilet and washing facilities were second to none, there was plenty of room, immaculate and fresh. One downside, if it does rain it does retain water, our tent faced a bit of a flood but in true form everyone rallied round and a good holiday was had by all. It hasn't put us off – we will be heading back again soon.

Comment by L. May from Fife

Stayed for a couple of nights in June with my 3 kids (10, 8, 6). Campsite is IMMACULATELY maintained, and toilet block is SPOTLESS. There is a great play park, football pitches, pitch 'n' putt, leisure centre and the Forfar town centre all within a few hundred yards. Only minor gripe is that the warden was a wee bit over-zealous in not allowing the kids to kick a ball back and forth. However, that's minor, and I would definitely recommend this site.

Comment by John from Dunfermline
Type of accommodation: Tent

- **TOTAL PITCHES:** 70
- **OPEN FROM:** end March to early November
- **UNITS ACCEPTED:** tents, motorhomes and touring caravans
- **FACILITIES:** large central facility block with ample toilet and shower facilities; disabled facilities; electric hookups throughout caravan and camping area; Elsan disposal for emptying of chemical toilets; showers; laundry; pets accepted
- **CHILD-SPECIFIC FACILITIES:** baby-changing; heated toilet block; local nature trails; play park
- **LOCAL CHILD-FRIENDLY ATTRACTIONS (FREE):** Forfar Loch Country Park; nature trails; free local ranger events
- **LOCAL CHILD-FRIENDLY ATTRACTIONS (WITH A CHARGE):** Glamis Castle; Pictavia; Caledonian Railway; HM Frigate *Unicorn*; Montrose Basin Wildlife Centre; water sports within 8km; golf and fishing within 8km; RSPB reserve within 16km
- **POOR-WEATHER ACTIVITIES:** Glamis Castle; HM Frigate *Unicorn*; Caledonian Railway
- **NEAREST CHILD-FRIENDLY BAR/RESTAURANT:** several child-friendly restaurants and bars in Forfar

Kilvrecht Caravan and Camp Site

Kinloch Rannoch
Perthshire
PH16 5QA
Tel: 01350 727284
Website: www.scottishcamping.com/
kilvrecht

Kilvrecht Camp Site is located in the heart of Highland Perthshire close to the shore of Loch Rannoch and within Tay Forest Park. It is just 5km, on the south Loch Rannoch road, from the village of Kinloch Rannoch which has a hotel, a post office and a café. There is no longer a service station so fill up before heading along the road to the site.

The onsite facilities are basic but the woodland setting and its remote location make this a real adventure to get to and a fantastic setting for kids to explore. This is not a place for families looking for entertainment but for those who make their own.

There is no hot water in the facility blocks and no electric hookups so go prepared to be self-sufficient and enjoy it. There is a covered cooking and socialising area located over the burn if required and there are picnic tables onsite.

Fishing, forest walking and water sports are on your doorstep. The area is also great for trail and mountain biking and older competent cyclists can consider undertaking the 32km tarmac road loop of the loch, which is relatively traffic-free and flat and goes through stunning scenery. The loop also incorporates a clan trail which can offer regular breaks.

The site is signposted on the loch's southside road.

Who needs abroad, this is HEAVEN!

Reviews

Who needs abroad, this is HEAVEN!

This is as basic as it gets, running water only and toilets, but who needs more, my wife and kids have camped here twice now, the only drawback is the highland midges, but you learn to live with them, feeding them doesn't seem to be a problem. The scenery, the peace, the fresh air, we'll be back again and again, just please don't make it a commercial camp site like some bigger ones, this is true Scotland at its best, where else can you fall asleep under the stars to the sound of owls hooting and wake up to the sound of woodpeckers?

Comment by George and family
from Glenrothes
Type of accommodation: Tent

We go there every year now for the past 5 years, our kids love it, the people are very friendly, there are 3 or 4 set country walks – you can fish and the kids can play in the river. It's very cheap to camp – it's the best value for money anywhere. You can't beat it – we will be back every year.

Comment by Dave, Stacy and kids
from Edinburgh
Type of accommodation: Tent

Just come back from a weekend camping at Kilvrecht. 4 adults, 5 kids and a dog. Pick your own pitch. Fantastic quiet location, plenty of space for kids to run around and play without disturbing other campers.

Comment by Gilly Marshall
from Edinburgh
Type of accommodation: Tent

Had a great weekend here in May due to the huge variety of places to camp on this site from large open field, small wooded corner and lots in between. Very friendly and helpful staff, toilets very clean and no showers – great, who wants to wash while camping anyway! Brilliant walking around the area and for a half-day out the wee hill directly above Kinloch Rannoch is very hard to beat.

Comment by Keith Harper
from Edinburgh
Type of accommodation: Tent

- **TOTAL PITCHES:** 90
- **OPEN FROM:** April to October
- **UNITS ACCEPTED:** tents, motorhomes and touring caravans
- **FACILITIES:** onsite toilet block; cold running water; pets accepted
- **CHILD-SPECIFIC FACILITIES:** wildlife, including red squirrels, in the park
- **LOCAL CHILD-FRIENDLY ATTRACTIONS (FREE):** the site is the start of various walking and cycling routes
- **LOCAL CHILD-FRIENDLY ATTRACTIONS (WITH A CHARGE):** Activity Scotland sports activities; Blair Castle at Blair Atholl
- **POOR-WEATHER ACTIVITIES:** Activity Scotland outdoor sports activities from the Dunalastair Hotel in Kinloch Rannoch
- **NEAREST CHILD-FRIENDLY BAR/RESTAURANT:** hotels at Kinloch Rannoch within 5km

Blair Castle Caravan Park

Blair Atholl
Perthshire
PH18 5SR
Tel: 01796 481263
Website: www.scottishcamping.com/blaircastlecaravanpark
Email: mail@blaircastlecaravanpark.co.uk

Blair Castle Caravan Park is a site which families cannot resist returning to. Easily accessed from the A9 or by train, the site is great for families and offers numerous child-friendly opportunities on a well-managed and organised site.

Literally metres from the front of the site, Blair Atholl village offers a local shop, sit-in and takeaway food and a child-friendly local hotel with bar and restaurant. There is a small lade and burn, usually full of ducks, at the front of the site and the River Tilt runs along its eastern side. Often children are drawn to play down by the river and so families should ensure appropriate supervision of children in this area.

With 9 acres of space at its heart, five-star facilities and a relaxed family-friendly atmosphere, it is easy to see why Blair Castle Caravan Park is a favourite holiday destination. Adjacent to the historic landscape of Blair Castle, and surrounded by the spectacular mountain scenery of Highland Perthshire, the park is regularly visited by the native red squirrels and enjoys easy access to over 60km of Atholl Estate's network of waymarked trails and cycle tracks.

A range of family activities are available nearby, including 90-minute vintage tractor and trailer rides, pony trekking at the Blair Castle Trekking Centre (for over-12s) and nature-themed fun for all with the Atholl Estates Ranger Service. Nearby at Blair Castle there are regular children's tours of the castle as well as the ranger's family activities in the castle gardens and grounds.

Did not want to go home!

Reviews

- **TOTAL PITCHES:** 280
- **OPEN FROM:** 1 March to 30 November
- **UNITS ACCEPTED:** tents, motorhomes and touring caravans. Static caravans and log cabins are available to rent.
- **FACILITIES:** heated toilet and shower blocks with individual and family cubicles including disabled facilities; onsite shop; electric hookups; chemical disposal; laundry; pets accepted
- **CHILD-SPECIFIC FACILITIES:** large central reception which has games room with pool table, table tennis and arcade games; Internet gallery and Wii games console; miniature golf course and play park onsite; several child-friendly heated facility blocks onsite which include baby changing; wildlife including rabbits, ducks and red squirrels visit the park; some farm animals including sheep and Highland cattle are kept in enclosures
- **LOCAL CHILD-FRIENDLY ATTRACTIONS (FREE):** the site is at the start of various walking and cycling routes; Atholl Rangers service in the village offers various children's activities throughout the season for a minimal charge; the River Tilt is fenced off from the park; however there are various points where access can be gained down steps to the riverside walk
- **LOCAL CHILD-FRIENDLY ATTRACTIONS (WITH A CHARGE):** swimming pool at Blair Atholl; to the south, the attractions of Pitlochry and Perth; to the north, the Highland Folk Museum, the Highland Wildlife Park and Landmark Adventure Park
- **POOR-WEATHER ACTIVITIES:** Blair Castle; swimming at the local pool; the country life museum in the village
- **NEAREST CHILD-FRIENDLY BAR/RESTAURANT:** the local Atholl Arms Hotel serves food all day in its child-friendly Bothy Bar and restaurant. Food in the Park is a local sit-in and takeaway restaurant.

Portnadoran Caravan Site

Arisaig
Highland
PH39 4NT
Tel: 01687 450267
Website: www.scottishcamping.com/portnadoran
Email: holiday@arisaigcampsite.co.uk

Portnadoran, meaning 'bay of the otter' in Gaelic, is an institution to the families who visit here, many returning not just year after year but decade after decade. If you want to join the happy campers here, the advice is book early to avoid disappointment. Owners Alasdair and Audrey Macdonald are renowned for their hospitality.

Portnadoran is not only a haven for the sea life which lives in and passes its sandy shores, including otters, seals and child-friendly basking sharks, it also boasts the best sunsets over the Small Isles of Rum and Eigg and out to Skye. If you see one it will live in your memory for a very long time.

The site is situated on the golden sandy coast just 3km north of Arisaig village with hotels, a café, a post office, a store and a railway station. It offers all grass pitches surrounding an oval driveway. There are also several seasonal caravans and static homes onsite.

Best of all, it is only metres from the site to the safe, gently sloping beach with its many rock pools to explore. There are no child-specific facilities or play areas but if your children enjoy the outdoors, exploring with their imagination, and are water-confident they will love this place.

The site is ideal for those families who love swimming, kayaking or other water sports. Small boats can be launched from the site.

The site is located on a working croft which has chickens, ponies and farm dogs.

'When are we going back?'

Reviews

There may not be man-made facilities for children – if there were I'm sure they'd be deserted! The beach, rocks and pools kept children of all ages amused for days, not just hours! Even usually stroppy teenagers spent hours climbing, exploring and swimming.

For teenagers reluctant to leave technology & contact with the 'real' world behind them we were surprised to find a strong mobile phone signal! It was without a doubt worth the 8-hour drive to get there – we'll certainly be back!
Edited comment by the ROCs
from Northumberland
Type of accommodation: Tent

One of the best campsites for a family holiday. The beach and the walks, the sunsets and the Macdonalds. They have been doing this for 40 years or more, so they should be good at it by now. And the description is accurate, very customer-oriented and very good with kids … I remember being told that Portnadoran was Gaelic for 'home of the otter' by old man MacDonald too. I will be back soon with my wife and kids (Chinese) from Beijing to show them what dad used to do. I hope they enjoy it as much as I did and you will.
Edited from comment by Ken Moore (or as old Mac called me 'Wee Fife') from Beijing, China
Type of accommodation: Static

Fantastic campsite, well-run, very customer-friendly owners. Brilliant location next to beach and ideal for kids. Facilities pretty basic, but clean and more than adequate. My kids loved it and its good-value, old-fashioned camping, unbeatable if you get the weather!
Comment by Jason Clark
from Deanston (by Doune)
Type of accommodation: Tent

- **TOTAL PITCHES:** 30
- **OPEN FROM:** Easter to 15 October
- **UNITS ACCEPTED:** tents, motorhomes and touring caravans. Static caravans are available to rent.
- **FACILITIES:** toilet and shower block; electric hookups; chemical disposal; laundry; open campfires allowed on beach; pets accepted
- **CHILD-SPECIFIC FACILITIES:** wildlife and farm animals onsite
- **LOCAL CHILD-FRIENDLY ATTRACTIONS (FREE):** the site is right on the beach; rock pools, sandcastles and rock climbing occupy most children's days; children's play park in Arisaig village; sea fishing
- **LOCAL CHILD-FRIENDLY ATTRACTIONS (WITH A CHARGE):** Mallaig and District leisure and swim centre; Traigh golf course; boat trips
- **POOR-WEATHER ACTIVITIES:** Mallaig and District leisure and swim centre; Arisaig Land, Sea and Island Centre; Fort William by car or train
- **NEAREST CHILD-FRIENDLY BAR/RESTAURANT:** the local Knoc-Na-Faire bar and restaurant just over 1km. Café and hotels in Arisaig

Invernahavon Caravan Site

Glentruim
Newtonmore
Inverness-shire
PH20 1BE
Tel: 01540 673534
Website: www.scottishcamping.com/invernahavon
Email: enquiries@invernahavon.com

Invernahavon Caravan Site is a Caravan Club site but is open to non-members. It is beautifully situated in the very heart of the Highlands and just off the A9. Bounded by salmon and trout rivers, it offers breathtaking views of the mountains and forests, providing a wonderful base for seeing the Highlands. The site is ideal for families looking for a smaller and quieter site within the Cairngorm National Park. The site provides pitches with ample space and a large and safe play area for children. Onsite facilities are clean, modern and well maintained, with constant hot water.

If you are keen on outdoor or mountain sports this is an ideal location with access to hill walks, rock climbing, water sports and the Wolftrax mountain biking course at Laggan. For those who love nature there are bird sanctuaries and a wildlife park as well as the Cairngorm National Nature Reserve. Even a quiet walk through the woods and forests at Glentruim offers the chance to see many species including red deer, roe deer, red squirrels, pine martens, wildcats and buzzards. Often children are drawn to play and swim in the river and so families should ensure that they are appropriately supervised in this area.

The site is located just 4km south of Newtonmore, which can easily be accessed by national cycle route. It offers a well-stocked shop selling groceries and Calor and camping gas. Pets are welcome but must be kept under control at all times. Electric hookups are available, for which advanced booking is advisable. Proprietors are the friendly Susie and Kenny Knox.

Bitten by Invernahavon – not the wildcat or Wolftrax

Reviews

A lovely spacious site well laid out. Clean showers and toilets with plenty of hot water. Lovely views and only about three miles from Newtonmore – cycle track available for the walk or cycle. As others have said, do not miss the Highland Heritage museum. First class and free – a tremendous resource. We went three times – so much to see and do. Clan Macpherson museum also interesting – donations welcome but free too. Couple of nice hotels for food/drink. Local Co-op selling most foodstuffs and papers and Spar in the garage as you enter Newtonmore. We had our three-year-old grandson with us and he had plenty of freedom at this site.
Edited comment by Jim McCallum from North Ayrshire
Type of accommodation: Camper

Return visit for us to this site this summer and despite the weather was just as good as our first trip. Surrounding views difficult to beat and kids just love the open spaces of the play area and the den-making potential in the wooded areas! Site was much busier this time but still plenty of space that you are not pitching on top of your neighbours and toilets/dishwashing/laundry facilities all still v clean. Highly recommended.
Comment by T Troupes from Perth
Type of accommodation: Tent

Spent two fantastic nights at Invernahavon in June. We had two big tents and had the camping area to ourselves, the surrounding woodlands, riverbanks and the trim trail kept the kids happy for hours. Despite being close to the A9 the site is really peaceful. Onsite there is a small shop – stocks mainly tins/jars. There is a coffee shop approximately 1 mile away – you can walk along the old A9. We will definitely be back!
Comment by G Gang from Perth
Type of accommodation: Tent

- **TOTAL PITCHES:** 60
- **OPEN FROM:** end March to early October
- **UNITS ACCEPTED:** tents, motorhomes and touring caravans
- **FACILITIES:** heated toilet and shower blocks including disabled facilities; electric hookups; chemical disposal; onsite shop; laundry; payphone; pets accepted
- **CHILD-SPECIFIC FACILITIES:** child-friendly heated facility block onsite, including baby changing
- **LOCAL CHILD-FRIENDLY ATTRACTIONS (FREE):** near to the start of various walking and cycling routes including Laggan Wolftrax; river close by and access can be gained from the site; wildlife including rabbits and red squirrels; next to the site is Mains of Glentruim Farm, home to pedigree Highland cattle (visits to the farm can be arranged via the shop)
- **LOCAL CHILD-FRIENDLY ATTRACTIONS (WITH A CHARGE):** river fishing onsite; the Highland Folk Museum; Loch Insh and Loch Morlich watersport centres; the Highland Wildlife Park; Landmark Adventure Park with pony trekking and quad biking; loch fishing; Cairngorm mountain railway and skiing
- **POOR-WEATHER ACTIVITIES:** As above and Aviemore swimming pool
- **NEAREST CHILD-FRIENDLY BAR/RESTAURANT:** Several local hotels and eateries serve food all day in Newtonmore (4km)

Ballater Caravan Park

Anderson Road
Ballater
AB35 5QR
Tel: 01339 755727
Website: www.scottishcamping.com/
ballater
Email: ballater.caravanpark@
aberdeenshire.gov.uk

Ballater Caravan Park is situated centrally in the village of Ballater in Royal Deeside, on the eastern edge of the Cairngorm National Park. The site lies in an ideal location for families who enjoy the great outdoors and provides opportunities for hill walking and mountain biking in the Lochnagar and Deeside areas. The site offers stunning scenery with open views of the rugged hills. It is set beside the River Dee which is popular for fishing and canoeing. The golf course is also adjacent to the park.

Ballater village is on the Castle Trail and Victorian Trail and is home to the Highland Games attended by the Royal Family. The site is a short 300m walk to variety of shops, places to eat and services where most families will find their camping needs met.

The park has a children's play area, picnic tables and area for ball games. Horse riding, which can be arranged locally, and cycling are very popular activities; cycles are available to hire in the village.

The site is signposted from the village main street.

Campers should be aware that the River Dee runs down one side of the campsite and there is an area for crossing to the golf course. Care is required here and may pose a hazard to children not adequately supervised.

One for the outdoor enthusiasts!

Reviews

Fantastic site, honestly could say one of the best I've been to in Scotland. The warden Andy was a gem of a character, facilities might be a bit old (laundry) but they do the job. Noise levels at night were mostly kept as requested (no noise after 10.30pm), lovely flat pitches, plenty stand pipes & picnic benches. Couldn't ask for more. Plus the location. Site doesn't have a shop as such, but the warden did freeze my blocks for free and the town is only a 5 min walk away. Go to this site, you will love it. You do need a car, though, for most things outside Ballater are a short drive away.
Comment by John & Tracy
from East Kilbride
Type of accommodation: Tent

Great wee site. Extremely busy, but we had booked in advance. Ballater itself is set in a very scenic location on the banks of the River Dee, and is extremely busy with tourists. Excellent location to go walking in the surrounding hills. We will back there at some point soon.
Comment by Marty from Dundee
Type of accommodation: Tent

Great mixed site – statics plus touring – beside the Dee in lovely Ballater. If you don't know Ballater, it's a wonderful small town on Deeside near to lovely walking and on the Deeside Cycle Path. This side of the mountains is a lot drier (we had retreated here from the west coast when the forecast had turned awful) and no (well hardly any) midges. Easy walk into town – gourmet eating to pub food, wonderful shops and lovely atmosphere. Perfect.
Edited comment by Les Ellis from Hampshire
Type of accommodation: Camper

- **TOTAL PITCHES:** 52 touring with electricity and 40 tent or touring pitches without electricity
- **OPEN FROM:** late March to late October (check specific dates with the site)
- **UNITS ACCEPTED:** tents, motorhomes and touring caravans. Static caravans are available to rent
- **FACILITIES:** facility block offering toilet and showers, including disabled facilities; laundry; electric hookups; disposal point for emptying chemical toilets; onsite shop; pets accepted
- **CHILD-SPECIFIC FACILITIES:** baby changing; heated toilet block; local nature trails; play park
- **LOCAL CHILD-FRIENDLY ATTRACTIONS (FREE):** Countryside Ranger events locally and within Cairngorm National Park
- **LOCAL CHILD-FRIENDLY ATTRACTIONS (WITH A CHARGE):** Deeside Activity Centre (22km from Ballater) offers (among many other activities) quad biking, kart racing and paintballing; golf on local course; fishing on the River Dee; Aboyne swimming pool
- **POOR-WEATHER ACTIVITIES:** TV room onsite; small free library in reception; Deeside Activity Centre; Aboyne swimming pool
- **NEAREST CHILD-FRIENDLY BAR/RESTAURANT:** a selection of child-friendly pubs and restaurants are available in Ballater

Deeside Holiday Park

South Deeside Road
Maryculter
Aberdeen
AB12 5FX
Tel: 01224 733860
Website: www.scottishcamping.com/
deeside
Email: deeside@holiday-parks.co.uk

Deeside Holiday Park is situated in Royal Deeside but is also within easy travelling distance of Aberdeen. This family-run holiday park offers a safe, friendly haven for children to enjoy the freedom and fun of the outdoors. The onsite adventure play area is a great place for kids to play, make friends on the long summer days and get to know the Deeside ducks in the onsite duck pond. When the weather is not so good the site offers an indoor games room with play equipment including table tennis, table football, a pool table and a TV lounge.

The touring pitches are spacious and are situated in well-landscaped surroundings sheltered by trees and shrubs. They are mainly hardstanding but there are some level grassed pitches within the site. Tent campers are accommodated in a lovely level and sheltered grassed area where electric hookups are available.

Close to the park there are lots of outdoor activities for children and their families and the site is also located only a few miles from Deeside Activity Centre where there are numerous sports on offer. For younger children the magical world of Storybook Glen is very close by for a visit.

Within Aberdeen city there are a number of child-friendly places of interest including the beachfront amusement park, ice rink and leisure centres. So whether you are looking for entertainment onsite or off, Deeside has a great deal to offer your family on their camping trip together.

Kids persuaded us to stay for two extra nights

Reviews

Campsite brilliant for kids. We booked for a week camping, but kids persuaded us to stay for two extra nights. If hadn't had to go to work would have stayed longer. Park and games room is a great meeting place for kids to make friends. Staff are kind and very helpful. Facilities are excellent. Will definitely return.
Comment by Steve Courtney from Dundee
Type of accommodation: Tent

We often come here for the weekend with our motorhome. Bus stop over the bridge and up the hill (10-min walk). Regular buses take you right into Aberdeen city centre. Also over the bridge is a fantastic cycle route which takes you right into Aberdeen and to the park (a flat six-mile ride). Our family have also stayed in the lodges which are lovely and very reasonably priced. Children's Storybook Glen Park within walking distance. Excellent site.
Comment by the Robertsons from Angus
Type of accommodation: Camper

Every year we come here about 3 or 4 times. It's a good break from the house and it's nice as no-one bothers you. We stay in the overflow field which is great for the kids. The shower rooms are excellent too; the only thing to recommend is to maybe put some sets of stairs from the park to the field beside the tent pitches. Other than that can't wait to go back again. Good fun.
Edited comment by Mrs Carolanne Bain from Aberdeen

Nice and peaceful campsite. This was our first stop and found it perfect. Will come again!
Comment by Bissett family from Cambs
Type of accommodation: Tent

- **TOTAL PITCHES:** 115
- **OPEN FROM:** all year round; booking in advance is always recommended, especially during peak periods
- **UNITS ACCEPTED:** tents, motorhomes and touring caravans. Static caravans and wooden lodges are available to rent.
- **FACILITIES:** toilet and shower block providing facilities; specially adapted disabled toilet and shower room; electric hookups; disposal for emptying chemical toilets; onsite shop; laundry; pets accepted
- **CHILD-SPECIFIC FACILITIES:** baby changing; heated toilet block; play park; indoor games room; TV lounge; enclosed duck pond
- **LOCAL CHILD-FRIENDLY ATTRACTIONS (FREE):** Aberdeen and Stonehaven beaches; Duthie and Hazelhead parks; Balmedie Country Park
- **LOCAL CHILD-FRIENDLY ATTRACTIONS (WITH A CHARGE):** locally: Storybook Glen; Deeside Activity Centre. Aberdeen: Cadonas Fun Fair; Stratosphere Science Centre. Stonehaven: outdoor swimming pool. Banchory: soft bear play centre; Royal Deeside Railway
- **POOR-WEATHER ACTIVITIES:** Aberdeen: beachfront leisure centre; cinema; Stratosphere Science Centre
- **NEAREST CHILD-FRIENDLY BAR/RESTAURANT:** The Old Mill Inn (400m)

Haughton Caravan Park

Haughton Country Park
Montgarrie Road
Alford
Aberdeenshire
AB33 8NA
Tel: 01975 562107
Website: www.scottishcamping.com/
haughton
Email: haughton.caravanpark@
aberdeenshire.gov.uk

This child-friendly site is located within the 80 hectares of Haughton Country Park which is run by Aberdeenshire Council and located on the outskirts of Alford. Alford lies 40km west of Aberdeen and is accessible by public transport.

Originally a private estate with the Mansion House at its centre, the estate is primarily made up of accessible woodland, the riverside and a grassy area with ornamental planting. A narrow-gauge train runs through the park to the golf course and village during the summer. Within the caravan and country park area are several equipped play areas, a riverside trim track, woodland walks and a picnic area. Fishing is available on the River Don – permits can be purchased onsite or online. The site can be busy with visitor traffic but it operates a one-way system and a speed limit for cars. This is a riverside park so there are natural hazards including the River Don and a pond as you would expect in such a natural setting.

In reception there is a games room, putting hire, board games hire, free book exchange and a children's nature corner with quizzes, pictures to colour and sheets with items to find and record.

Haughton is on the Castle Trail and in the village of Alford. Within easy walking or cycling distance are the transport museum, dry ski slope, indoor swimming pool, village railway and heritage museum which will keep the children amused indoors or out whatever the weather.

Full steam ahead to Haughton!

Reviews

Excellent site for camping, loads of space and you can pick your pitch. Plenty of play parks for kids as well as putting green, pool tables and table tennis. Huge park with lots of paths and nature trails, so if you've got bikes, take them with you. Showers and wash facilities are clean and all you could ask for. If you camp next to the big house be prepared for the dawn chorus from the coos and the local jackdaw population (a real back to nature feel). No shop on site, but a pleasant 15 min walk takes you into town for all your necessities, and you have to try the local butcher's huge burgers on the barbie: MAGIC.
Comment by the Lamb Family from Markinch, Fife
Type of accommodation: Tent

Stayed here last weekend, great site located in Haughton Country Park. Plenty of walks and very well kept. We pitched our tent in the walled area (Tent Site 3), nice and sheltered and close to the park for the kids and also the toilets and washing facilities. We enjoyed it and so did the kids, we will be back.
Comment by Marty from Dundee
Type of accommodation: Tent

Have been here lots of times last year with lots of friends, liked it every time, kids love it too. Nice clean site – would recommend to anyone. Been up there already this yr and going back again soon.
Comment by Mrs Carolanne Bain from Aberdeen

- **TOTAL PITCHES:** 12 tent with electricity, 70 tent/touring without electricity and 100 touring with electricity
- **OPEN FROM:** end March to end October (changes yearly so check with site for specific dates)
- **UNITS ACCEPTED:** tents, motorhomes and touring caravans
- **FACILITIES:** heated toilet and shower block, including disabled facilities and baby changing; shop; laundry; games room; no open campfires allowed but BBQ stands available to hire; pets accepted
- **CHILD-SPECIFIC FACILITIES:** baby changing; heated toilet block; wildlife onsite; local nature trails; play park
- **LOCAL CHILD-FRIENDLY ATTRACTIONS (FREE):** regular ranger events onsite and children can access free fishing; waymarked nature trails and picnic areas
- **LOCAL CHILD-FRIENDLY ATTRACTIONS (WITH A CHARGE):** Alford swimming pool and leisure centre; outdoor activity centres; pony trekking; fishing
- **POOR-WEATHER ACTIVITIES:** swimming pool and Grampian Transport Museum in Alford; many visitor attractions in Aberdeen
- **NEAREST CHILD-FRIENDLY BAR/RESTAURANT:** several family-friendly restaurants, bars, bistros and cafés in Alford village

Glenmore Camping and Caravanning Site

Forest Holidays
Glenmore
Aviemore
Inverness-shire
PH22 1QU
Tel: (bookings) 0845 130 8224; (site) 01479 861271
Website: www.scottishcamping.com/ glenmore
Email: info@forestholidays.co.uk

Children of all ages will enjoy this site as it is situated in the heart of the beautiful Cairngorm National Park, with all the adventure you would want literally at your door. The site lies just 11km, by road or new cycleway, from Aviemore. Aviemore village is easily accessed by car from the A9 and has a mainline train station; it offers all the services a family may require. Glenmore Camping and Caravanning Park is an ideal choice for those wishing to stay on a site in the heart of the National Park and within its Caledonian Forest.

Native wildlife includes deer, otters, red squirrels and pine martens, while golden eagles or ospreys may be spotted overhead. Lying at the foot of the magnificent Northern Corries of the Cairngorms and on the gently shelving sandy shore of the majestic Loch Morlich, this site offers the visiting family the most spectacular setting. The whole family can take part in walking, sailing, windsurfing, canoeing or fishing.

The site is large, open and fairly informal with a mix of tent, caravan and motorhome pitches in most areas. It allows you to choose your pitch at quieter times but be aware that the site can become quite congested and very busy during peak periods.

This site is open all year round to make the most of its proximity to Cairngorm Mountain which is home to one of Scotland's most extensive ski areas. It is run jointly by the Caravan Club and Forest Holidays.

Location, location, location!

Reviews

Great location with Cairngorms on doorstep and even has a beach on shores of Loch Morlich – kids loved it. The new shower block is a welcome addition. Clean and modern and in a central location. The site would have got 5 stars if they had a better kids' play area but with all that natural beauty about can't complain. Not far from Aviemore and all its facilities. If taking kids head for Landmark in Carrbridge – great day out and great value.
Edited comment by John Madden from Dunfermline

Stayed for a weekend. Superb location in woodland next to loch. Kids spent a lot of time exploring the campsite, and we went for walks and cycles (plus water sports) for the whole weekend, leaving the van in situ (excellent meal at Glenmore Lodge, too, by the way). Found the staff very welcoming and the facilities excellent. On the expensive side, but worth it – we'll definitely be back.
Comment by Adam from Inverness.
Type of accommodation: Camper

Only 3 stars for kids' facilities but they don't need facilities here as there is so much to do. Onsite beach on Loch Morlich is great. Big site but facilities big enough to cope, modern and clean. We were unlucky with noisy neighbours but warden dealt with the situation tactfully. Good base for enjoying all the National Park has to offer.
Comment by Liz and Cameron from Ayrshire

- **TOTAL PITCHES:** 206
- **OPEN FROM:** all year round
- **UNITS ACCEPTED:** tents, motorhomes and touring caravans
- **FACILITIES:** two large heated toilet and shower blocks; disabled facilities; electric hookups; chemical disposal point; shop and café just offsite; laundry; pets accepted
- **CHILD-SPECIFIC FACILITIES:** baby changing; heated toilet block; wildlife onsite; local nature trails; children's play area
- **LOCAL CHILD-FRIENDLY ATTRACTIONS (FREE):** great sandy beach and forest areas to explore; nature trails ideal for biking and walking; Forestry Commission Ranger events
- **LOCAL CHILD-FRIENDLY ATTRACTIONS (WITH A CHARGE):** clay pigeon shooting (12+) and quad biking at Rothiemurchus near Aviemore; Landmark Adventure Centre at Carrbridge; Ace Adventure river rafting, mountain biking and hire, sailing and water sports at Loch Morlich and Loch Insh; archery; Aviemore swimming pool and adventure club including soft play
- **POOR-WEATHER ACTIVITIES:** the Imagination Workshop (arts and crafts studio), Aviemore; Safari by Land Rover; Waltzing Waters (indoor water show) at Newtonmore; Strathspey Steam Railway
- **NEAREST CHILD-FRIENDLY BAR/RESTAURANT:** small café and shop just offsite, bar meals available at Glenmore Lodge; the child-friendly Hilton Coylumbridge Hotel (8km); wide choice of eateries in Aviemore

Grantown on Spey Caravan Park

Seafield Avenue
Grantown on Spey
Highland
PH26 3JQ
Tel: 01479 872474
Website: www.scottishcamping.com/
grantown
Email: sandra@caravanscotland.com

Grantown on Spey, the capital of Strathspey, should not be missed as a holiday destination when visiting Scotland as it is conveniently located for a variety of child- and family-friendly activities and experiences ranging from wildlife to adventure. The site is located less than 1km north-west from the town's main street and is well organised with excellent 5-star facilities. Grantown the town has a variety of services, including shops, cafés and takeaways, a leisure centre and hotels. Grantown's Caravan Park offers you and your family the ideal site from which to take advantage of all that is offered locally in the town and further afield.

The site is well laid out and tents not requiring electricity are located in a separate area of the park. It has an informal feel in that it does not have specific pitches, allowing the ground covered to be rotated. Everyone can therefore enjoy some fresh grass on which to pitch. The site also offers picnic tables adjacent to your pitch for your convenience. Beautiful surroundings attract an incredible array of birdlife. Set against the backdrop of the Cairngorm Mountains, the site is also convenient for the Speyside Way and exploring further Cairngorm National Park.

Facilities include a new toilet block with full underfloor heating and all modern conveniences. For families these include a special toddler washroom and changing facilities for babies.

The site is Caravan Club affiliated and also offers caravan Super Pitches (minimum of 9m wide) with their own Sky TV box, water and waste disposal on pitch and 16-amp electricity.

Couldn't believe how good this site was

Reviews

Stayed one week my wife and two kids aged 8 and 5 (both boys) on our first camping trip for a long time and couldn't believe how good this site was. The toilet block was immaculate with superb facilities. The kids' play park was great for the kids who met loads of new friends and despite there being a lot of kids the site was really quiet and peaceful at night. We were on the lower pitch in our tent with no electric hookup as the site was so busy, price of 22 quid a night seemed rather on the expensive side for a tent but I'd rather pay the extra for a wonderful site and would pay it again. The location of the site means you are close to all the local shops, bars, takeaways etc. Overall though the site really made our holiday most enjoyable and we will most certainly return next summer.
Edited comment by Happy Camper from East Kilbride.
Type of accommodation: Tent

Enjoyed our stay here in the late spring. Facilities could not have been cleaner. We have no children and enjoy peace and quiet and were pleased to see that amongst the caravanners, there seemed to be a designated area for those with children nearer to the play area (which looked very good quality) while those who want peace and quiet can pitch far far away! Helpful warden. Lovely walks nearby. Will be back in the spring to try and find capercaillie! Really excellent site.
Comment by Johnny Boy from Fife, Scotland
Type of accommodation: Caravan

Probably one of the best campsites we've ever camped on. Toilet/shower facilities are second to none – they're almost brand new with underfloor heating and even have music piped through them. Scenery is magnificent. Great play area for kids and a football area too. We pitched our six-berth tent with lots of room to spare. This is also a dog-friendly site. The wardens are so friendly and we look forward to camping here again in the near future.
Edited comment by Graham Meiklejohn from Banff

- **TOTAL PITCHES:** 100
- **OPEN FROM:** 26 March until 30 October each year
- **UNITS ACCEPTED:** tents, motorhomes and touring caravans. Wooden wigwams are available to rent.
- **FACILITIES:** modern toilet and shower block with disabled facilities; electric hookups; disposal point for emptying chemical toilets; laundry; games room; pets accepted; wi-fi
- **CHILD-SPECIFIC FACILITIES:** baby changing; heated toilet block; toddler washroom; wildlife onsite; local nature trails; play park
- **LOCAL CHILD-FRIENDLY ATTRACTIONS (FREE):** cycling, walking and nature trails
- **LOCAL CHILD-FRIENDLY ATTRACTIONS (WITH A CHARGE):** clay pigeon shooting (12+) and quad biking at Rothiemurchus near Aviemore; Landmark Adventure Centre at Carrbridge; Ace Adventure river rafting, mountain biking and hire, sailing and water sports at Loch Morlich and Loch Insh; archery; swimming at Craig Maclean leisure centre in Grantown on Spey
- **POOR-WEATHER ACTIVITIES:** swimming at Craig Maclean leisure centre; the Imagination Workshop (arts and crafts studio), Aviemore; Safari by Land Rover; Waltzing Waters (indoor water show) at Newtonmore; Strathspey Steam Railway
- **NEAREST CHILD-FRIENDLY BAR/RESTAURANT:** several to choose from in the town

Cannich Caravan and Camping Site

Cannich
By Beauly
Strathglass
Inverness-shire
IV4 7LN
Tel: 01456 415364
Website: www.scottishcamping.com/
cannich
Email: enquiries@highlandcamping.co.uk

For many years Cannich Caravan and Camping Site has proved to be one of the most popular child-friendly sites. Recommended by many families because of the combination of owner Fay's attention to customer service, its great location and its close proximity to the village facilities, it appeals to families with an interest in the outdoors, nature and scenery. The site is situated at the head of Glen Affric (often referred to as the most scenic glen in Scotland) and close to Cannich village. The site's location also offers access to the nearby Glens of Cannich and Strathfarrar. All these areas are great for families and kids who like to walk, explore and go mountain-biking.

Further afield, families can also go by car to Drumnadrochit and the historic Urquhart Castle which sits on the shore of Loch Ness. From here you can attempt to spot Nessie, the elusive monster. The site itself covers six acres and, set within Scots pine and birch woodlands, provides a peaceful retreat. It is excellent for young children as it is located away from busy roads. It offers children an onsite play park and plenty of space for bike riding. The site is located just five minutes' walk from the village, which has a well-stocked shop and child-friendly pub.

Pitches are flat and many have their own picnic benches. There is indoor dishwashing and a TV room for kids. The site is now open all year for camping and tourers and has a heated toilet/shower room. There is also an onsite café which is open every day from 9am to 5pm.

A little treasure!

Reviews

We have just returned from three nights camping at Cannich – our first camping experience – and could not have chosen a better site. We phoned first and were impressed by the helpfulness of the staff. On arrival we were taken on a stroll around the site so we could pick the spot we liked best to pitch our tents. The setting is stunning and waking up to the scenery around us and the numerous rabbits was something our children will always remember! The café was excellent and coffee/cakes were to die for! The kids really enjoyed the playground, pool table in the TV room and hiring out bikes for the day. We also enjoyed the local area and waterfall trails nearby. We were there at what surely must have been their busiest time of the year and we still felt that there was plenty of room around us and the availability of shower facilities was fine. They were also clean and free to use. We were sad to leave and have come back with great memories of such a well-organised and friendly campsite in a stunning location.
Comment by Angie Freeman from Glasgow
Type of accommodation: Tent

We stayed on this site for two nights, during our 'Grand Tour' of Scotland. We had wanted to visit Loch Ness, and after looking at other sites near to the Loch, we decided that they just weren't up to our standard – we drove to this site, with the aid of our Camping Scotland map, and found what can only be described as a 'little treasure'! Our kids loved the play park and the fact that we had breakfast in the fabulous café right onsite! The loos were always clean, as were the showers. Very helpful staff too.
Comment by Lisa
from South Wales, UK
Type of accommodation: Camper

Beautiful location. The family that run the site are very friendly and helpful. We spent two very relaxed nights there last July. Would recommend it to anyone. The scenery is out of this world, and if you're into big trees it's heaven. Will be back.
Comment by Tentastic from London

- **TOTAL PITCHES:** 43
- **OPEN FROM:** all year
- **UNITS ACCEPTED:** tents, motorhomes and touring caravans. Wooden wigwams and static caravans are available to rent.
- **FACILITIES:** showers; laundry; disabled facilities; TV room; café; electric hookups; open campfires; pets accepted; wi-fi
- **CHILD-SPECIFIC FACILITIES:** baby changing; heated facility block; play park; TV lounge
- **LOCAL CHILD-FRIENDLY ATTRACTIONS (FREE):** play park; nature trails highlighting local animal and birdlife and ranger-led walks
- **LOCAL CHILD-FRIENDLY ATTRACTIONS (WITH A CHARGE):** local swimming pool; pony trekking; bike hire
- **POOR-WEATHER ACTIVITIES:** swimming pool; bird-watching at Abnachan Forrest; the city of Inverness can be accessed in less than an hour by car
- **NEAREST CHILD-FRIENDLY BAR/RESTAURANT:** child-friendly restaurant and bar (1km)

Aden Caravan Park

Mintlaw
Peterhead
AB42 5FQ
Tel: 01771 623460
Website: www.scottishcamping.com/aden
Email: aden.caravanpark@aberdeenshire.gov.uk

Aden Caravan Park enjoys a wonderfully peaceful location in rural Aberdeenshire near Mintlaw, a small village located just 11km west of Peterhead. The site is part of the extensive country park which is home to the Aberdeenshire Farming Museum, a restaurant and a craft shop. Mintlaw is central to the area known as Buchan. The village offers a variety of services including convenience stores and places to eat including the prizewinning Mintlaw Chipper and Restaurant. The village was historically serviced by the Maud to Peterhead railway and had its own station. Nowadays the old dismantled line provides a haven for wildlife and is part of the Formartine and Buchan Way (a long-distance walking route).

The country park has won many prestigious awards including a Green Flag award for being one of the country's best green spaces. The site itself is set in a woodland area within the 87 hectares of the country park and contains extensive grassy areas for games and picnics, a small loch and a riverside area along the banks of the River Ugie. The country park has many lovely walks including around the lake area where you can feed the resident ducks, and many events arranged by the countryside rangers. It has a large children's play area and children can visit the tree house. There is also a seasonal ice-cream kiosk situated in the main car park.

The caravan park contains a children's play area and picnic area. It is an extremely well-laid-out site with a well-maintained facility block.

What a fantastic find!

Reviews

Stayed here and had a magic weekend. Plenty to do for the kids – on and off site. Outdoor gym, swans in lake. Toilets were kept clean at all times and owners very friendly. Will definitely be going back this summer.
Comment by Leah from Aberdeen
Type of accommodation: Tent

Stayed here with friends for the first time. What a fantastic find! The staff are so friendly and helpful, nothing is ever a bother. The play park is adequate, but a 3-minute walk through the beautiful woodland and there is a park the children would have spent all day in given half a chance. Going back again in September. Would definitely recommend to families.
Comment by JA from Stirling
Type of accommodation: Tent

We stayed here a couple of years ago and thought it was fantastic. Everyone really friendly and welcoming. The kids want to come back so will be returning this year.
Comment by McCord Family from Meigle, Perthshire

Enjoyed this site. Very busy with family camping but it did not make it too noisy at night. We would go back. Staff very friendly and helpful.
Comment by May Fletcher from Aberdeenshire

- **Total pitches:** 48 touring with electricity, 25 tent/touring without electricity
- **Open from:** late March to late October – check specific dates with site
- **Units accepted:** tents, motorhomes and touring caravans
- **Facilities:** toilet and shower block; disabled facilities; electric hookup; disposal for emptying chemical toilets; shop; laundry; pets accepted
- **Child-specific facilities:** baby changing; heated toilet block; local nature trails; play park
- **Local child-friendly attractions (free):** local Ranger events; working farm museum within heritage centre in country park
- **Local child-friendly attractions (with a charge):** Peterhead leisure centre offers swimming, a health and fitness suite, a coffee bar and vending service, Amazone soft play activity area, a four-court games hall, and indoor climbing wall, a multi-purpose practice hall and community/toddlers area
- **Poor-weather activities:** heritage centre and farming museum; Peterhead leisure centre; Aberdeen and its attractions
- **Nearest child-friendly bar/restaurant:** there is a restaurant within the country park and the local garden centre serves food. Other places to eat can be found in Mintlaw.

Banff Links Caravan Park

Banff Links
Banff
AB45 2JJ
Tel: 01261 812228
Website: www.scottishcamping.com/banff
Email: banff.caravanpark@aberdeenshire.gov.uk

On the Seaside Award winning beach at Banff Bay, Banff Links Caravan Park is a popular site with families looking for a seaside holiday next to this small town. The site is located on the coast away from busy roads between the coastal towns of Whitehills and Banff. Banff, the larger of the two, is less than 2km away and situated on the banks of the famous River Deveron. The town offers many shops, hotels, cafés and takeaways. On the other shore of the Deveron lies Macduff, a small but busy fishing port with its own marine aquarium.

The site is located right on the beach which is popular with surfers and kite flyers. Caution and/or supervision are advised when children are on the sands. A well-equipped play area lies next to the caravan park.

From Banff it is easy to explore by car the coastal villages of the north-east including Pennan, the setting of the famous *Local Hero* film. There are boat trips available locally to take you dolphin/puffin/whale spotting, and you may even be lucky enough to catch a glimpse of a dolphin from the beach. The park is ideally situated for walking and cycling. The grounds of nearby Duff House have an adventure playground, a play park and a picnic area.

There are several local golf courses in addition to the Duff House Royal Golf Club, including the Royal Tarlair Golf Club, situated in Macduff. Excellent freshwater and sea fishing are available locally.

I know what we will be doing next year.

Reviews

Park is located right on the beach. The play park next door is perfect for all ages of children. The toilets and showers are kept clean and tidy. A short walk along the beach takes you right into the centre. It's peaceful, friendly and gr8 priced, ideal location and not too large, so booking early is a must. Love it – a favourite
Edited comment by the Isles family from Dundee
Type of accommodation: Tent

This site is right on a lovely beach. The kids loved it and spent most of their time in the sand or water. There was also a brilliant play area at the other end. The facilities were clean enough and showers were hot. Tent spaces are limited so I'd advise booking but the tents are right at the top of the site so it is quiet. We would definitely recommend it for campers of any age
Edited comment by Karen from Dundee
Type of accommodation: Tent

First time in a caravan since I was a child ... Wanted a hassle-free holiday for us and our two children (9 and 3) ... so decided on a caravan. Lovely beach, lovely sea views, great play park ... within days my eldest had a group of friends – we didn't see her for most of the day ... I even felt safe letting my 3 year old play in the park for a short while without adult supervision ... We didn't actually go anywhere much in the area apart from MacDuff aquarium which was good value and filled the only rainy afternoon we experienced. Banff has several shops – I'd recommend the 'spotty bag shop' – East side shopping centre (I forgot to take my fleece and got one here at a good price). For food it has a Tesco (smallish), a Coop and a Somerfield and there was a small shop onsite that sells a range of things – from milk to buckets and spades ... and water bombs(!). There are lots of places to eat in Banff and a couple of places in Whitehills ... everything we had was good value and tasty ... Downsides: the sea is very very cold – a wet suit is almost essential ... and it was windy (we bought a wind break!). But it is the best family holiday we have been on ... and I know what we will be doing next year.
Edited comment by Lucy from Fife.
Type of accommodation: Static

- **TOTAL PITCHES:** 60 touring with electricity, 24 tent/touring without electricity
- **OPEN FROM:** late March to late October – check specific dates with site
- **UNITS ACCEPTED:** tents, motorhomes and touring caravans. Static caravans are available to rent.
- **FACILITIES:** toilet and shower block, including disabled facilities; electric hookups; disposal point for emptying chemical toilets; laundry; pets accepted; open campfires allowed on beach
- **CHILD-SPECIFIC FACILITIES:** baby changing; heated toilet block; local nature trails; play park
- **LOCAL CHILD-FRIENDLY ATTRACTIONS (FREE):** great beach to explore with large park adjacent to caravan park with well-equipped play area
- **LOCAL CHILD-FRIENDLY ATTRACTIONS (WITH A CHARGE):** Macduff Marine Aquarium with touch pools where children can handle starfish etc; Banff swimming pool
- **POOR-WEATHER ACTIVITIES:** Macduff Marine Aquarium; Banff swimming pool; Harley's Leisure Centre in Macduff with soft-play facilities, a tenpin bowling alley and a restaurant
- **NEAREST CHILD-FRIENDLY BAR/RESTAURANT:** Banff, nearby Whitehills and Macduff have a variety of cafés, bars and restaurants

Sands Caravan and Camping Park

Sands Holiday Centre
Gairloch
Wester Ross
IV21 2DL
Tel: 01445 712152
Website: www.scottishcamping.com/sands
Email: info@sandscaravanandcamping.co.uk

Sands Caravan and Camping Park is situated close to the village of Gairloch (5km) on the beautiful west coast of the Highlands. It offers unsurpassed views of the Isle of Skye and Outer Hebrides. It is the ideal location for a child-friendly holiday.

Gairloch village has shops, cafés, hotels and a post office, while the site itself has many services which mean you may not even need to leave the site.

The spacious 55-acre site is flanked by farmland on two sides and the sea on the other. As a result it offers plenty of space even when busy. The main attraction for families is the large golden sandy beach, which is ideal for many types of water sports or just watching the sun go down while toasting marshmallows on a beach campfire. For children the site is a natural adventure playground where they can spend their time on the mountainous sand dunes playing games of hide and seek or exploring the rock pools on the seashore which are teeming with sea creatures such as crabs, winkles and limpets. A small burn runs through the site where kids can skim stones or race little boats down to the sea. There is also a play park which includes the popular flying fox, swings, slides, tunnels and a balance trail.

The caravan and camping park is run on an informal basis. It is divided into two main areas, one for camping and the other for caravans. The camping area allows you the freedom to choose your own pitch. There are sheltered spots amongst the sand dunes or others with a view across the Minch to the Isles. Wherever you set up, the award-winning beach is just a stone's throw away.

Sands = relaxation!

Reviews

My family love this site, like so many folk before; we were only staying for 1 night – that ended up 4 nights. The kids only came back to the van for food (the way it should be) between the beach, games room and general adventure. Hubby loved the scenery and walks, and he found the ground great for the awning pegs. The 4-legged members of the family had a number of choices of great long walks (dog owners please pick up and bin the dog mess). Sands have a great laundry room with spin dry, washers, tumble drier, irons + boards, plenty of sinks, lovely clean toilets and fab showers that are powerful and hot unlike so many campsite showers. In our opinion 'Sands = Relaxation' – why not go and see for yourself.
Comment by Paws from Fife
Type of accommodation: Camper

Smashing! What a splendid place! The location is excellent, right next to a fantastic beach that was perfect for a relaxing evening walk with the hound before putting the baby to bed. There are few rules and common sense is allowed to prevail, which all of our fellow campers had in abundance. Tents have one area, caravans another and campers can go where they like; the only request is to keep at least 20ft from your neighbour (fair enough!). The facilities were very good, and the old onsite chip van was a lot better than expected. To simply sum up this site, we booked for two nights but stayed for five and didn't want to leave! In fact, we may just have to go back again before the end of summer!
Comment by Coose
from North Yorkshire
Type of accommodation: Camper

- **TOTAL PITCHES:** 200
- **OPEN FROM:** April to October – booking only required during July and August
- **UNITS ACCEPTED:** tents, motorhomes and touring caravans. Wooden wigwams and static caravans are available to rent.
- **FACILITIES:** three toilet and shower blocks providing ample facilities; disabled facilities; 70 electric hookups in caravan and camping area; Elsan disposal for emptying chemical toilets; a purpose-built motorhome service point; Highland wi-fi hotspot; shop; laundry; games room; pets accepted; open campfires allowed
- **CHILD-SPECIFIC FACILITIES:** baby changing; heated toilet block; cooking shelter/campers' kitchen; wildlife onsite; local nature trails; play park
- **LOCAL CHILD-FRIENDLY ATTRACTIONS (FREE):** sea fishing from pier and rocks; loch and river fishing for campsite customers; great beaches to explore
- **LOCAL CHILD-FRIENDLY ATTRACTIONS (WITH A CHARGE):** swimming pool (12km); leisure centre (5km); boat trips (6km); pony trekking (6km)
- **POOR-WEATHER ACTIVITIES:** indoor games room onsite; swimming pool leisure centre and museum offsite
- **NEAREST CHILD-FRIENDLY BAR/RESTAURANT:** three child-friendly restaurants/bars within 5km

Horgabost Campsite

Horgabost
Isle of Harris
HS3 3HR
Tel: 01859 550386
Website: www.scottishcamping.com/
horgabost

This is a great campsite which offers an experience close to wild camping but with a brilliant Hebridean twist. Families who venture here will not find all the facilities associated with conventional sites but those on offer will ensure that your stay is pleasant. What you will take from this site are memories of turquoise seas, white sands and a Caribbean landscape from one of our less visited areas.

Horgabost is located on the Isle of Harris which is not, as is commonly believed, a separate island from Lewis but rather the southern landmass attached to the larger Isle of Lewis. Harris has a more mountainous rugged landscape than its northern neighbour and also boasts wonderful beaches. Horgabost is located around 20km south of Tarbert from where Calmac Ferries run to Uig on the north of the Isle of Skye. Tarbert is the main settlement on Harris and offers a variety of shops, hotels and cafés. Occupying the most southerly position on Harris lies Leverburgh (15km) from where Calmac Ferries run to Berneray, connected by causeway to North Uist. Leverburgh also offers services but these are less extensive than those of Tarbert.

For many years Horgabost beach, Traigh Niosaboist, was a coastal common grazing area which was used by passers-by as a picnic area and informal campsite. Because of the pressures on the land the site was closed to campers for several years during the 1990s before being opened up again and now is an official site. It is set just beyond the dunes that front the beach and is directly opposite the island of Taransay (featured on the BBC *Castaway* programme).

Possibly the best campsite in the world ...

The campsite is set on machair grazing land and is run by Richard and Lena, who regularly visit to ensure visitors have a pleasant stay. It is an ideal location for exploring the whole island and to come back to for a beautiful summer sunset. Apart from the small facility block there is also a small beach shop open in the evenings with a mobile shop visiting on Tuesdays and Fridays.

Located just over 1km to the north is Luskentyre beach, which has consistently been rated Britain's best beach and one of the world's top 10.

Reviews

Possibly the best campsite in the world...

Spent a single night here. In a word – unbelievable. The scenery is quite stunning. A simple coastal camp site is now not enough after camping at Horgabost!! Camped 10 feet from the beach, white sands, blue skies, aquamarine sea then stunning mountains across the sound of Taransay. Razorbills, terns, mergansers and seals fishing, just offshore. Light till midnight, perfect! I can't wait to return.
Comment by Paul Barker from Toft Hill, County Durham
Type of accommodation: Tent

Magnificent views and location on the beach and just off the main road. I was there camping for 3 days with two young children and they had the time of their lives! Giving a star rating for children's facilities doesn't really apply because the beach, stream and surrounding machair are exactly what the children liked. Any 'playpark' type facilities would greatly detract from the experience and their own imaginations for play. Made wee friends and had brilliant (safe) fun. We camped near the toilets/shower/washroom/car park area overlooking the beach and stream. Ideal for supervising the wee ones, close to toileting and near to the car for transferring the gear. Very clean, friendly and unspoilt with relaxed set-up. Nearest shop (it's a good one) is in Leverburgh about 10–15 mins drive, so just plan your provisions. We had our little dog with us and there were many others with dogs – no problems, they also love it here.
Comment by Geoff Elder from Lewis
Type of accommodation: Tent

- **TOTAL PITCHES:** 50
- **OPEN FROM:** May to October
- **UNITS ACCEPTED:** tents, motorhomes and touring caravans
- **FACILITIES:** toilet block; small beach shop; visiting mobile shop (Tuesdays and Fridays); pets accepted
- **CHILD-SPECIFIC FACILITIES:** brilliant local beaches
- **LOCAL CHILD-FRIENDLY ATTRACTIONS (FREE):** beaches
- **LOCAL CHILD-FRIENDLY ATTRACTIONS (WITH A CHARGE):** Ionad Spòrs Eilean na Hearadh (Isle of Harris Sports Centre) in Tarbert with swimming pools, sauna and fitness centre
- **POOR-WEATHER ACTIVITIES:** play cards and games in your tent; visit the Isle of Harris Sports Centre
- **NEAREST CHILD-FRIENDLY BAR/RESTAURANT:** child-friendly café/hotel in Tarbert (20km)

Clachtoll Beach Campsite

Near Lochinver
Sutherland
IV27 4JD
Tel: 01571 855377
Website: www.scottishcamping.com/
clachtoll
Email: mail@clachtollbeachcampsite.
co.uk

Clachtoll Beach Campsite is a touring caravan and camping site in Sutherland, north-west Scotland. The site is 10km north of Lochinver and has proved consistently popular with families who are seeking a 'get away from it all' site. The area next to the site is renowned for its outstanding natural beauty and spectacular land and sea scapes.

Lochinver is the closest town and has a variety of eateries and shops. There is also a welcoming visitor centre and local leisure facilities.

The campsite covers an area of approximately 2.5 acres and is entirely grass. It has a golden sandy bay on its doorstep perfect for keeping children entertained. There is a well-maintained facility block but what attracts children and families is that this site offers a natural play park for which all you need to bring is your imagination. The bay has a wonderful, gently shelving, horseshoe sandy beach with rock pools and around the site wildlife abounds.

On arrival visitors are asked to report to wardens Jim and Ishbell who are perfect hosts and are always proactive in helping with any camping issues. They will help you to find a suitable pitch.

White sandy beach and crystal clear water

Reviews

Our first camping holiday with kids. Owners so helpful and even provided matches which we forgot. Loads of space onsite. Campsite was 'full' but still loads of space/privacy. Facilities spotless, cleaned twice a day. Beach perfect. No formal play area but kids didn't need it. Couldn't recommend it more highly.
Edited comment by J. Williams from Perthshire
Type of accommodation: Tent

We spent two nights here and were greeted as soon as we arrived by Jim & Ishbel. Any questions were answered and help was offered to put up our tent. Plenty to do and keep our 5 year old busy with the rock pools and playing in the water. Highly recommended site. Facilities were clean and tidy.
Edited comment by Diane, Euan, Aowyn, Kwuari and Bonnie from West Lothian
Type of accommodation: Tent

Thank you, Jim, Ishbel, Cath and Charlie, the best campsite wardens you could ever wish to meet – always on hand to help, from putting up tents to charging kids' Nintendos. Spent a week here – toilet and shower block warm and always clean at any time of day. Tent pitches well spaced, as much room as you would ever need. This is a get away from it all holiday – limited mobile phone signal but a payphone on site if you really want to be found and when you see the white sandy beach and crystal clear water you'll understand why. There's no playground so it was great to see kids mixing with each other playing rounders, tennis, sandcastle competitions, enjoying the beach and rock pools: that's the best facility any campsite can offer.
Edited comment by The Martins from Scotland
Type of accommodation: Tent

- ■ **TOTAL PITCHES:** 40+
- ■ **OPEN FROM:** Easter to September – booking is advisable during July and August and at all times for the limited serviced pitches
- ■ **UNITS ACCEPTED:** tents, motorhomes and touring caravans
- ■ **FACILITIES:** facility block (including toilets and showers which are disabled friendly); dishwashing sinks; laundry; chemical disposal point; public telephone; 12 serviced pitches with water and electric hookups; dogs welcome provided they are kept on a lead at all times on the campsite
- ■ **LOCAL CHILD-FRIENDLY ATTRACTIONS (FREE):** safe sandy beach; local nature trails and coastal walks; ranger's hut; organised events including sandcastle competition in August and guided walks April to September; sea and loch fishing; two parks in Lochinver
- ■ **LOCAL CHILD-FRIENDLY ATTRACTIONS (WITH A CHARGE):** Assynt Leisure Centre in Lochinver offers indoor sports facilities and organised events during school holidays and at weekends and has a café and Internet suite. Lochinver Tourist Information Centre has a shop, displays and activities for children including the heron watch project with nest camera. Kayaking can be arranged locally.
- ■ **POOR-WEATHER ACTIVITIES:** Assynt Leisure Centre (Lochinver); Culag Wood (Lochinver) offers a walk with surprises in a sheltered location
- ■ **NEAREST CHILD-FRIENDLY BAR/RESTAURANT:** Two child-friendly restaurants and bars within 8km.

Pickaquoy Centre Caravan and Camping Park

Muddisdale Road
Kirkwall
Orkney
KW15 1JG
Tel: 01856 879900
Website: www.scottishcamping.com/
pickaquoy
Email: enquiries@pickaquoy.com

Orkney offers a great experience for families. Not only does it have beautiful beaches and towering sea cliffs, it also has the most ancient monuments per acre of land in Western Europe, many of which are easily accessed by families and easy to explore. These include the Neolithic chambered cairn of Maeshowe, the standing stones of Ring of Brodgar and the stone-built settlements of Skara Brae, all of which hold World Heritage Status. Alongside these there are many other sites to visit and explore, including Pictish brochs and Viking settlements.

The site is on the outskirts of Kirkwall, near supermarkets, the town and the pier from which ferries leave daily to the North Isles for those wishing to island-hop whilst in Orkney.

The Pickaquoy Centre Caravan and Camping Park is Orkney's largest camping and caravan park and has been extensively developed over many years to make it a great family site. The site lies on the doorstep of the modern Pickaquoy Centre which provides a variety of activities and adventure for children of all ages. This is an ideal site for families who love activities; if you are looking for a site in Orkney and especially in Kirkwall it is hard to beat what this site has to offer.

There are a total of 81 pitches both hard and grass standing. The facility block also includes a lounge area, kitchen and laundry room.

The site is located near a main road and not far from the island harbour area and sea.

Everything comes to them that wait

Reviews

We visited at the end of June, and loved the site and the island. The best facilities on any site we have ever visited in the UK and in Europe. Spotlessly clean all the time. Even has a lounge for tenters wanting a comfy seat and somewhere to socialise. Sheltered site, as it can be windy. Shops and ferries very near, short walk into Kirkwall town.
Comment by Sue & Stewart from Cheshire UK
Type of accommodation: Caravan

Just back from this campsite and could not fault it in any way, ultra clean and modern facilities, very helpful staff, very good space for each pitch/caravan. Shops in abundance just down the road. What a place Orkney is, lots to do and see for all ages and plan to return in the very near future. Everybody should see this great island.
Comment by Mr M Allan from S.W. Scotland
Type of accommodation: Tent

This is easily the best site we have visited. The location and facilities are first class and it deserves the highest rating.
Comment by C.S. Hepburn from Maryburgh
Type of accommodation: Camper

- **TOTAL PITCHES:** 81; this includes 28 hard stands with electricity, 3 grass stands with electricity and 50 grass-only stands, including sheltered tent areas
- **OPEN FROM:** 1 April to 31 October – booking is recommended during July and August
- **UNITS ACCEPTED:** tents, motorhomes and touring caravans
- **FACILITIES:** family-friendly modern facility block (with twelve separate shower/washing cubicles, four toilet/washroom units and one family/disabled shower/toilet unit); disabled facilities; electric hookups; chemical waste disposal point; showers; laundry; lounge room; pets accepted
- **CHILD-SPECIFIC FACILITIES:** baby changing; heated toilet block; local nature trails; play park
- **LOCAL CHILD-FRIENDLY ATTRACTIONS (FREE):** play park onsite and nearby skate park; beaches close by for swimming, sea fishing and exploring
- **LOCAL CHILD-FRIENDLY ATTRACTIONS (WITH A CHARGE):** boat trips from harbour, leisure centre, cinema and swimming pool
- **POOR-WEATHER ACTIVITIES:** leisure centre has swimming pool, badminton and tennis courts, five-a-side pitches, health zone, gym, Jungle World for 3 to 8 year olds, cinema and café
- **NEAREST CHILD-FRIENDLY BAR/RESTAURANT:** several child-friendly restaurants and bars in Kirkwall

Skeld Caravan and Camping Site

Skeld Waterfront
Skeld
Shetland
ZE2 9NL
Tel: 01595 860287
Website: www.scottishcamping.com/
skeld
Email: scottjandj@tiscali.co.uk

Shetland, the most northerly of the Scottish Isles, is famously linked to its Scandinavian history and its close association with the sea. Thankfully Vikings no longer call here but you and the children can easily discover Shetland seafaring and Nordic history. Skeld Caravan and Camping site offers families the opportunity to enjoy some of the best camping facilities while overlooking a busy marina.

The site is located at the waterfront in Skeld on the western side of the Shetland mainland. It is a lovely quiet, sheltered, safe and friendly site located away from any main roads. The site is run as a community venture and is staffed by volunteers who give all visitors a friendly welcome, offer their local knowledge and try to accommodate most requests from site visitors.

The site has a new purpose-built facility block which is ideal for families as it offers all the usual facilities along with a kitchen area with seating and access to cooking utensils and dishes, a fridge, a toaster and a microwave.

There are two areas of hardstanding pitches, one of which overlooks the water and marina. The camping area is made up of flat, well-maintained grass which doubles as an area on which families can play ball games. There are also several picnic tables throughout the site. Onsite visitors have access to outdoor games equipment and there is an indoor area with board games. At night the site is well lit and during the day children will be keen to visit the site's own wildlife hide from which many

Gem of a campsite

visitors have viewed the local birds, seals and otters. Within easy walking distance (5 mins) there are two children's play parks. As the site is located at the waterfront parents must be responsible for their children at all times. Children under 16 are not permitted on the marina unless accompanied by an adult.

Reviews

This gem of a campsite fully justifies a five star rating and deserves to be better known. The facilities are excellent, including showers, laundry and kitchen facilities all of which are scrupulously clean and maintained by dedicated friendly local volunteers. The site is perfectly situated by the sea, adjacent to a small marina and even includes a hide equipped with binoculars and reference material and from which sea otters can be spotted. If you're going to Shetland, make a point of visiting this well-run campsite.
Edited comment by Gwen
from Edinburgh
Type of accommodation: Camper

We stayed here for one night and it was fantastic. The facilities (toilets, showers, washing up, microwave etc.) are excellent and immaculately clean – as are the public facilities as well. There is a hide on site where you can watch the seals, birds and otters if you are very lucky. The local community is rightly very proud of what they have achieved and they provide a very warm welcome.
Edited comment by Amanda from London
Type of accommodation: Camper

An excellent site, stunning views and perfect location for exploring the Shetland Islands. The camp site hosts Jim and Josephine go over and above normal standards with help with sightseeing info. The site is new and fresh – a wonderful place to relax and just enjoy.
Edited comment by Wendy from Southampton
Type of accommodation: Tent

- **TOTAL PITCHES:** 19
- **OPEN FROM:** all year round
- **UNITS ACCEPTED:** tents, motorhomes and touring caravans
- **FACILITIES:** showers; electric hookups; chemical disposal; laundry; pet friendly; campfires by arrangement
- **CHILD-SPECIFIC FACILITIES:** baby changing; disabled-friendly heated toilet block; campers' kitchen; play parks close by; wildlife hide onsite
- **LOCAL CHILD-FRIENDLY ATTRACTIONS (FREE):** two play parks; beaches at Raewick; fishing from pier; Michael's wood; picnic and play areas at Airth, Da Gairdins at Sand; Bonhaga art gallery and café
- **LOCAL CHILD-FRIENDLY ATTRACTIONS (WITH A CHARGE):** swimming pool and leisure centre at Airth; pony-riding lessons at Weisdale
- **POOR-WEATHER ACTIVITIES:** swimming pool and leisure centre at Airth; Bonhaga Mill; Lerwick Museum; board games in the amenity building
- **NEAREST CHILD-FRIENDLY BAR/RESTAURANT:** Bonhoga restaurant/café, Burrastow hotel/restaurant and the café at Airth public hall (all 20km)

Choosing your site and planning ahead

This book will have whittled your choices down a bit while still offering you a great variety of child-friendly sites to choose from. Only you will really know what will be the best choice for your kids and what you are all looking for from a camping trip. The choice of site may depend on one or more of the following factors: your levels of experience; who will be in your camping group; your likes and dislikes; the time you have available; and your access to transport. We hope that whichever site you choose, this book will help to make your camping trip a more enjoyable and memorable experience.

Practice makes perfect!

Always practise putting your tent up and trying out your stove at least once before you go camping. If you have a motorhome or caravan ensure you know how it works or get a demonstration from the hire company before you leave. This will enable you to familiarise yourself with the process of pitching and allow you to check everything is there, which will save you time and potential embarrassment onsite. Pitching instructions for tents are usually found inside the tent bag, either sewn into the fabric or as a loose piece of paper. Some more modern tents now come with DVDs that will demonstrate how to pitch your tent.

Weather

Think about where you are going and get a decent weather forecast for your trip. The BBC and Met Office provide reliable forecasts. It is worth being aware that the east of Scotland has much lower average rainfall than the west but that the weather in Scotland can vary significantly across the country on any particular day. Weather from low-pressure systems tends to bring unsettled conditions of wind and rain while high pressure generally brings lighter winds, clearer skies and more settled conditions. Wind and rain together can have a chilling and demoralising effect on the non-prepared camper so plan ahead for this eventuality. Remember too that weather in Scotland changes quickly and that very wet mornings can become glorious afternoons. Plan things that you can do on wet days (follow the suggestions in this book) so that you have alternatives to staying onsite. The sound of rain on the outside of your tent, caravan or motorhome can bring a reassuring sense of well-being when you are warm and dry inside so make sure you keep the essential sleeping areas and bedding dry.

Should we book ahead?

ScottishCamping always recommends that you contact the site in advance if you wish to use their services (before 8pm if phoning) as sites are constantly changing their facilities and can be fully booked at both peak and non-peak times. Please also ensure that you state your requirements when you call as sites operate different policies towards group sizes and compositions, the units they accept and pets.

Our advice is to inform the site of the following: the size of your tent(s), motorhome or caravan; who is in your group (including pets); what you are looking for from the site and any other special requirements your group may have. This should help the site allocate you the pitch best suited to your needs and spare you a wasted journey to a site that will not accept your unit type, family group or pet.

On arrival at the site

Go to reception to book in; in the event that reception is not staffed when you arrive there are usually instructions posted outside. If this is the case, follow the instructions and if allowed, have a look. Some sites will allocate you a pitch on booking or arrival while others will be less formal and allow you to find your own pitch. See p. 86 for advice on what to consider when choosing your pitch.

Camping equipment checklist

This is a list of what we would recommend you pack as a minimum. As well as taking those items listed below, your children's checklist should include sunscreen and a hat, waterproofs and wellies, small familiar toys and games and a torch. You may also wish to consider their taking their own rucksack which could hold a bug viewer with wildlife identification cards or books and children's binoculars. The usual favourites of fishing nets or rods, a kite and a bucket and spade also usually come in handy.

Tent (see also p. 76)

If tent camping we strongly recommend that you purchase a tent with a flysheet or outer sheet, given the variable weather in Scotland. As its purpose is to keep out the elements a tent consisting of one sheet is likely to leak and/or build up condensation. We also advise that you have insectproof or midgeproof netting over ventilation points, a sewn-in ground sheet and a down-to-the ground all-round flysheet.

Other considerations when buying a tent include weight; storage space; ventilation; cooking area/porch; and entrance design. For wild camping or camping in seasons other than summer, we recommend you seek advice from a reputable outdoor shop on design and weight considerations.

Practise putting your tent up before you go as it could be windy or raining when you arrive and you could end up as the site entertainment. Pitch your tent end on to the prevailing wind if possible. If pitching your tent on a slope, pitch it not across but in line with the slope in order to sleep with your head slightly uphill.

Sleeping bag (see also p. 78)

There are a variety of types to choose from. Make sure that your sleeping bag is suitable for the predicted weather conditions and that you air it regularly to keep it moisture-free. It is also worth considering a sleeping bag liner to keep your bag clean and extend its use.

Stove (see also p. 81)

There are many types of camping stove, including those of different weights and using different types of fuel. Seek advice from a reputable outdoor shop and try the stove out before you go.

Camping mat (see also p. 80)

These are available in a variety of lengths and thicknesses and are very useful for giving extra insulation and comfort on cold, stony or hard ground.

Fuel and matches/lighter

Your stove isn't much use without them.

Cooking utensils, cutlery and washing-up essentials

Saucepans, plates and cutlery. Tin/bottle opener/penknife, pot scourer, washing-up liquid, towels

Food (& coolbox if needed)

See the recipes section, p. 107.

Appropriate clothing

Plan for poor weather! Waterproof/windproof clothing, waterproof shoes or boots, warm clothing that you can layer to keep you warm.

Spare clothing

Bin liners

These are useful to put wet gear in.

Insect repellent, sun cream, hat

You have heard of the midge – be prepared! Scotland looks glorious in the sunshine but you will need hats and sunscreen for everyone.

Water carrier

Torch and spare batteries

Personal toiletries, medicine, toilet paper, wipes and towels

First-aid kit

Weather forecast

Camping table and chairs if needed

What type of tent, sleeping bag or stove?

The information below on tents and sleeping bags has been supplied by Vango, a company with a long and illustrious history in designing and manufacturing outdoor products.

Tents (see also the checklist on p. 74)

The following are some key points to remember when buying or borrowing a tent

- Consider the size of tent you require. It might sound obvious, but many first-time campers don't spend enough time researching this. Bear in mind the space you'll need for bags or luggage, the communal space available such as a seating/eating area and the layout of the sleeping space. If you are a family with older children, they might prefer their own space or 'pod'.

- How much time are you willing to spend pitching your tent? If you have younger children, time will be at a premium as you need to keep an eye on them and keep them entertained while the tent is going up.

- How long will you be camping for? If you are just going to be heading off for a weekend or short break you don't want to have to haul a large and heavy tent pack with you. There are plenty of weekend tents available that can sleep families of four to six people. If you are going away for longer, then you might be happier to invest in a larger tent with more features and space.

- When and where are you going camping? If you plan to travel abroad with your tent, bear in mind the changes in weather and temperature you might encounter. A well-ventilated tent is vital wherever you pitch up and a waterproof tent will be essential for any domestic campers.

- What kind of accessories and furniture are available and are they compatible with your tent? Those fashion-conscious campers among you might be interested to find out if there are colour-coordinated chairs, carpets and accessories to match your tent.

Here is some basic information on the structure of the tent.

The framework of the tent consists of poles. These are commonly made from fibreglass and aluminium for modern designs, although steel and wood are still used for particular styles. The poles can be positioned in one of two places to hold the structure:

- inside the flysheet, allowing the fly to compress the poles and hold them in place better. Both the inner sheet and the flysheet are connected to the poles.

- outside the flysheet with the fly hanging on the pole structure, then an inner hanging inside the flysheet. This method makes for a quicker shelter and allows both the inner sheet and the flysheet to be pitched together in most instances.

Over the years, the configuration of the poles has changed in line with developments in materials used. With the introduction of the flexible pole the 'tunnel' tent was born. Tunnel tents allow for greater useable space inside.

Straightforward tunnel tents tend to be a bit simpler to erect and many of them go up fly first (which can be an advantage in Scottish wet weather). They also tend to have slightly more internal volume because of their steep end walls.

Geodesic tents use a set of mutually supporting poles and so tend to be far more stable in wind and much less reliant on guying out to give them shape. Semi-geodesic tents tend to have more of an angled tent roof than tunnel tents as they taper back from the front, where a two (or more) poled tunnel tent has more of a flat roof and thus more of a constant internal height.

Sleeping bags

Sleeping bags are designed to maintain maximum warmth during the cooler hours of the night. When choosing a sleeping bag a number of factors should be considered:

Temperature range

This is the range at which the sleeping bag best performs. Vango provides a suggested temperature range and most of the range is tested to the EN standard, which provides temperature limits for each bag. Select a sleeping bag appropriate to the expected weather conditions using the comfort temperature range as the most important criterion. We suggest that if you expect temperatures close to the lower limit of the comfort temperature listed for a sleeping bag, you should consider moving up the range to the next warmest model, just in case you meet unexpected conditions or are ill, for instance.

Alongside temperature ratings some manufacturers still grade their sleeping bags on season ratings. As temperature ratings are generally for the wider market it is important to reconsider these with Scottish conditions in mind. The following is only a guide:

- A 1 season bag is for summer only. As a rule these are not really suited to Scottish summer conditions.

- A 2 season bag refers to a summer/spring bag and is generally considered much more suited to our warmer Scottish summer conditions

- 3 season bags are for spring to autumn and are suited to early and late summer in Scotland. They will be too warm in better Scottish summer conditions.

- 4 season bags cover most conditions when the temperatures remain above freezing. Given the variation in temperatures during the spring and autumn in Scotland it would not be uncommon to call upon the properties of a 4 season bag. Remember temperatures can drop to freezing and below during the spring and autumn which is for most families the beginning and end of the camping season.

- 5 season bags are for extreme conditions and the worst of the Scottish winter during which camping with children would not be recommended.

Obviously these seasonal ratings are not as reliable as temperature ratings as they are more general. If you have any queries on the type of bag to buy go to a reputable outdoor specialist.

Pack size

These vary according to the construction method and components within the sleeping bag. An expedition bag will have a smaller pack size for the same temperature than a sleeping bag for leisure use, as the construction and filling is more technical. Most Vango sleeping bags come with compression sacs which can be used to reduce the overall pack size for transit.

Weight

This is very closely linked to pack size as lighter components are often used in more technical bags.

Filling

There are two categories of filling: down and synthetic.

Down has a very good warmth-to-weight ratio but requires more care. The method of holding the down filling is crucial to the thermal properties of the final bag. Using the incorrect method will result in a poorly performing bag. **Stitch-through** is when the down is held between the shell and lining fabric. This method is not used on high-performance bags. **Box wall** is when the down is held in box-shaped chambers that provide the best space for the down to loft. This method reduces the cold spots. **Trapezoidal** is similar to box wall, except that here the walls are slanted to ensure maximum loft and fill from the down, the wider angle in the corners allowing better fill. **Omega construction** is used on the bags from Ultralite up and provides great body hugging and maintains maximum warmth both on top of and around the sides of the body. **TES** (Thermal Embrace System) uses elasticated thread in the lining to enable the sleeping bag to hug your body. This allows you to move freely when sleeping while the inner lining fits snugly around you. As the lining is encouraged towards you, it increases the loft between the inner and outer layers and reduces the amount of air around the body, resulting in greater insulation and more warmth.

Synthetics are improving all the time and can be used in various ways to improve insulation; however the insulation properties of synthetic fabrics decrease when wet. **Single layer construction** is when one layer of filling is used and either the lining or the shell fabric is stitched to the filling. Both can be stitched but this method can reduce the performance of the bag. This method is not used on high-performance bags. **Offset double layer construction** is when two layers of filling are used and are laid offset to each other and separated by a layer of non-binding mesh called scrim. This method reduces the cold spots. **TLS** (Thermic Loft System) makes use of a layering technique which combines classic synthetic insulation with a new interlocking lattice construction to produce a highly effective thermic insulation system.

Shape

The two basic shapes are **mummy**, providing a better body-hugging fit with less dead space, and **square**, providing more room within the bag and usually found at the lower end of the range.

User features

Bags are designed to be easy to use and fit the user well. Key features to look out for are: anti snag zips, internal security pocket, multi cord hood adjustment, shoulder baffles and lining fabrics.

Camping mats

The most common types of camping mat include:

Foam: these are the most common type and are made from a closed-cell foam construction; these mats are relatively thin and give minimal protection from the ground but they are lightweight and cheap.

Self-inflatable: these are a more modern alternative. They have a self-expanding and inflatable centre sandwiched between durable outer layers and can provide a mattress up to a couple of centimetres thick. These mats are usually heavier and cost more but they provide better comfort and insulation. They may sometimes need to be topped up by blowing into a small valve to increase the pressure and thickness.

Fully inflatable: these are similar to the inflatable beds or lilos you may have at home. They provide a better sleeping platform for some but they are bulky and heavy to transport. You will also need to carry a pump to inflate these.

Stoves

Some official sites will allow you to cook on open fires, but this is the exception rather than the rule and it is generally accepted that you will do your campsite cooking on a stove. A stove is therefore an essential part of your family camping kit. Stoves are dangerous, as they reach extreme temperatures and use very flammable fuel sources. Because of this, all children need to be supervised around them at all times. Older children can be taught to use stoves safely but should never be left to cook on a stove unsupervised. There are many different types of stove on the market, varying in fuel type, weight, convenience of use, cost and stability. Which you choose will depend on the type of camping you are planning to undertake, the composition of your group, your budget, whether an adult or child will be involved in cooking and what you intend to cook. Never use a stove inside your tent and always try your stove out before you go camping so you are familiar with its operation.

Here are some of the more popular choices:

Family camping stove

These are two-burner stoves that run on camping gas. These are generally for use when car camping as they are too heavy to carry, but if you have your own vehicle, several people to feed and the space they are worth considering.

Benefits	Drawbacks
stable	heavy and large stove and gas bottle
multi burners	expensive
can include grill	can be badly affected by wind

Trangia or similar methylated spirit burner

These are lightweight stoves which compact down to take up little space. Older children can develop cooking skills on these when appropriately supervised. All children require to be shown how to cook on these types of stoves as the lack of a visible flame during daylight can cause confusion and this can pose significant risks if refuelling. They come supplied with a variety of pots and collapsible handles. A separate fuel bottle is required.

Benefits	Drawbacks
cheaper	difficult to regulate temperature
lightweight and stable	can be difficult to see flame in daylight
effective in moderate wind	single burner

Single gas backpacking stove

These stoves are cheap and easy to use. You will, however, need to carry your own pots separately. They can be unstable on uneven ground and may be less efficient in the wind. Newer versions use heat exchangers to increase heat transfer.

Benefits	Drawbacks
lightweight	unstable on uneven ground
run on lightweight gas canister	can be top-heavy when using heavy pots
newer versions less affected by wind	older versions affected by wind

Multi-fuel stove

These are generally specialist backpacking pieces of equipment. The fuel needs to be pressured by pumping the fuel storage bottle or container. They are very efficient and are the fastest-heating stoves. They are generally stable and accessories such as windbreaks can be bought for them.

Benefits	Drawbacks
fast and efficient when boiling water	can require regular maintenance
stable	can be expensive
can use a variety of fuels	complicated for the beginner

BBQs and open fires

Only cook on a BBQ or open fire if your campsite permits their use. If BBQs or open fires are your preferred cooking method then you must contact your chosen site in advance. While there is no better way to cook than getting back to nature, open fires can cause problems if not appropriately managed. BBQs need to be raised well above the ground otherwise they will scorch the grass; this may not be evident initially but will result in dead and brown patches a few days later – a campsite owner's nightmare. This problem causes sites to ban their use. If you are building an open fire consider the use of a fire pit or similar to prevent damage and always source your wood or fuel with consideration. Small fires can be as efficient as large if managed effectively and can be a really fantastic cooking experience for children to witness and participate in. Toasted marshmallows, sausages, baked potatoes or bananas cooked in foil are exciting cooking experiences for children.

NB Don't forget your (waterproof) matches, lighter or fire stick and never put hot pans directly on the grass as this leaves burn marks and will infuriate the campsite owner!

Site rules and etiquette

Most campsites will have some rules and generally they are there to keep campers happy. Although our list is not exhaustive it gives a general idea as to what to expect. Remember that some sites will have written rules, while others will not but will expect you to show a degree of common sense about what is acceptable onsite. Some sites do not accept groups or pets, while others take couples only. There are also sites close to roads that do not accept children. It is always better to check ahead with your chosen campsite than to arrive and be disappointed.

Here are some general rules which you will encounter at most sites:

- The site has the right to ask you to leave at any time if you break site rules.

- Most sites have speed limits of 5–10 miles per hour to ensure safety. Remember that children are often playing near tents and caravans. It is usual for sites to not allow vehicular access between the hours of 10pm and 7am in order to reduce noise. Some have parking areas as an alternative.

- Children should be supervised by their parents.

- Most sites will not allow open fires and will ask that disposable BBQs are not placed on the grass or on tables. Some sites do not allow disposable BBQs at all, usually because of previous irresponsible campers. If using a stove do not place hot pans or pots directly onto the grass.

- Tents and caravans/campervans should be spaced at least 6 metres apart in case of fire.

- Many sites accept dogs but they should be kept on a lead at all times and should not be allowed to foul the campsite. Owners should clean up after their dogs.

- Washing dishes and clothes is not allowed in the toilet blocks and hot water should not be carried away. Use the laundry facilities or dishwashing areas.

- Most sites will expect everything to be quiet by 11pm and that at all other times noise will be kept to a minimum to avoid disturbing other site users. Some sites have wardens ensuring that this policy is adhered to.

- Most sites accept groups but check ahead. Some sites will have a separate area for organised groups of young people etc.

- You are expected to leave the facilities as you found them, cleaning up after yourself. If they are dirty this should be reported to the owner/warden.

What to consider when choosing your pitch

On arrival it is recommended you consider the following before pitching up.

Not all sites allow you to choose your pitch and may allocate you one on arrival. When the site is not full it is worth negotiating to have a look around in order to identify what would be best for your group. The time you spend doing this may be worth it in terms of your enjoyment later. Remember where you are put at first can be subject to change when other campers move on.

When looking round the site you may wish to consider its layout and consider where the nearest water source is, how close you need to be to the facilities and where other families are pitched (and whether you wish to be part of this group). Think about areas or paths where there might be noise, such as from passers-by.

Along with the site layout you may also wish to consider other physical factors including the ground. When considering a grass pitch look at the ground and the grass as it can give you vital information. Well-worn patches or yellow grass should generally be avoided to allow the grass to recover but do not rule out all barer areas as often a barer pitch indicates that it is frequently used and favoured. Remember that if it rains heavily water will gather in hollows and so look for telltale signs such as watermarks and boggy ground (the latter may also be identifiable by rougher, reed-type grasses).

Choose a pitch on higher ground if possible. Think about the effects of wind and consider how you can shelter from it. You may wish to look for a pitch on the site that offers a degree of shelter from prevailing winds; many sites have grown trees to provide windbreaks. A general rule is not to pitch under trees as rainwater will drip onto your tent long after the rain stops and there can also be the undesirable effects of sticky sap from buds, bird droppings and overhead dawn choruses.

Remember also that midges are more commonly encountered in damp areas free of breeze and out of direct sunlight.

Consider the lie of the land and its aspect. Try to pitch on flat ground where possible and think about where the sun might rise and set. A pitch on a west-facing slope will get sun in the evening and one on an east-facing slope in the morning.

If using a hardstanding pitch for a motorhome or caravan it is worth considering its distance from water supplies, electric hookups and facility blocks if you need them. Also consider how level the pitch is as this can affect your van's facilities, your sleeping positions and the efficiency of stoves and fridges. The use of levelling blocks can be used to remedy this. If you have an awning also consider where this will go.

No matter what type of camping you are involved in always treat your pitch well as others will need to use it after you. Leave it as you found it. In order to do this you can follow some of the following simple rules. When pitched on grass move your tent, motorhome or caravan every few days to allow the grass to recover. Never place hot pots or BBQs or pour hot water directly onto the grass as it will scorch and kill the grass, leaving patches of bare ground for those who follow. Always use the facility block or chemical disposal points for waste products.

Pitching your tent

The following hints and tips on pitching your tent have been supplied by Vango:

- Check the ground where you are intending to pitch your tent and remove any items that could damage your groundsheet.

- Try to remember to pitch your tent end on to the wind when possible.

- Check that the tent is pegged to the ground at all pegging points.

- All doors should be fully closed before pegging out your tent.

- All ties attaching the inner sheet and flysheet should be securely tied, but remember that you will have to untie any knots!

- All guylines should be pegged out and the pegs should be as secure as possible.

- Throughout your stay, check all guy and anchor pegging points.

- If the weather takes a turn for the worse, consider whether you should strike (take down) your tent. Note, however, that taking down your tent in bad weather could cause more damage.

- When you take down your tent, remember to pack it away in the reverse order of how you pitched it. You will also need to dry your tent if it is damp before storing it away.

What to know before you go family camping

The following information has been provided by campingexpert.co.uk

Taking the family camping is a great idea. It's a way of bringing everyone together and enjoying some good-quality time away from home and the daily routine. It's a chance to play and enjoy nature together. But there's more to it than simply packing everyone into the car and heading off to the country. For it to be successful requires thought and planning.

How old are your children?

There's certainly no upper or lower age limit for taking kids camping. A lot of people go with babies, although you'll have to make adequate preparations for sleeping and play. As all parents know, getting ready for any outing with a baby means assembling so much stuff that you feel like you're heading out for a month.

It's easier with older children but again there are things to consider. Just because you're in the great outdoors, it doesn't mean they can have complete freedom to go where they want. You need to consider animals and private property as well as potential hazards like water, which they might consider to be an adventure. You'll need to set limits on where and how far they can go, and be firm about enforcing your rules.

Family activities

One of the great joys of being on holiday together is being able to do things as a family. Do research on the area where you'll be camping. That will give you a chance to plan activities to satisfy everyone, whether it's exploring castles and stately homes, going to a petting zoo or a theme park, or simply walking in the country (and be careful on distance; you don't want to exhaust your kids and end up with them hating hiking). Allow plenty of time to simply relax and play, too – board games are an excellent way to pass an evening for everyone, as are simple card games.

Consider the practicalities

One important issue is where everyone will sleep. With young children you'll want them in the same tent as you, which means you'll have to plan for a tent that will allow you room to live alongside each other, in close proximity, for a few days. But at what age should they have their own tent(s)? That's up to you, of course, but they will want some independence. Teenagers may want to have their own tents and will probably want to socialise with others on the site, so you'll need to set deadlines, just as you would at home. How much freedom do you want to give them?

Unless your kids have spent time in the country, it's worth taking the time to educate them in the Countryside Code. They may feel they don't need this, especially if they're older, but it's still worthwhile. The rules are different from what they might have experienced, and so kids need to be aware of them and follow them. The same is true for etiquette. Treating people well is simply polite, of course, but in a campsite, where people are living closer to each other, it takes on even greater importance, with things like not making too much noise or dropping litter vital.

Take all these into account and spend time planning things and educating your children before you leave home and you'll end up having a camping holiday that everyone can enjoy – and the first of many together.

Camping activities with children

The following information has been provided by campingexpert.co.uk

The chances are that if you take the kids camping, they'll be so excited they'll spend a lot of time making their own fun. Kids will see camping as one big adventure and not only will they have a good time, they will also come back with more of an understanding about nature, wildlife and conservation, often without realising it.

Wildlife and nature

Most kids love wildlife. Even the smallest insect can be a source of endless interest so pick a site where you are likely to spot some wildlife. A torch will come in handy as it will enable the kids to spot animals that only come out after dark. Examine rocks, flowers, birds and so on and check out star constellations at night if the sky is clear enough.

Toys

Although you might get pestered by your kids before the trip about taking their computer games, you should try to discourage them from taking anything mechanical or electrical which might break or get damaged on the trip. Depending on their ages, kids can have a ball playing with sticks, rocks, leaves and flowers. Supplement these with balls, bats, Frisbees, buckets and spades and, for wet days, make sure you have plenty of board games, playing cards, pens, paper and crayons etc.

Sharing the experience

Kids will appreciate the whole camping experience even more if their parents join in with them and actively get involved. This needn't always mean playing games with them. Kids can have a lot of fun getting involved with the chores, which will give you some much-needed help too. Have competitions to see who can collect the most firewood or who can fill the water containers the fastest. Arrange a treasure hunt and see who can collect the items on the list in the shortest time. Hide and seek is always a favourite, too, especially in the woods.

Swimming

Before camping with children near to open water be sure that you and your children are familiar with water safety advice. If there is a loch or pond on or near the campsite, kids are likely to want to spend time splashing about in the water. It's always advisable to check with the site owner first to make sure the water is safe to swim in, to look out for any danger signs and to be aware of any hazards. If you're in a remote spot, an adult should check the water first. A good idea is to buy a pair of waterproof 'jellies' (rubber sandals). This prevents the kids from treading on anything dangerous in their bare feet.

All children should also be supervised if playing in or around water. Unfortunately every year there are serious incidents and deaths resulting from children and adults swimming in Scottish seas, rivers and lochs. Please be aware that the temperatures and speeds of Scottish waters can and do impact significantly on even the most able swimmers.

Fishing

If your kids enjoy fishing, bring a fishing net/rod or better still, share the experience of making one with your child.

These are just a few ideas. Knowing your kids' preferences will largely dictate the kinds of activities they'll want to participate in but whatever you decide to do, the more you join in with them, the more fun they will have. Camping for kids has many benefits - it is a physically demanding activity and their excitement and curiosity with the outdoors will mean that they'll inevitably get more exercise than usual. It is not only fun but educational and teaches them about the natural world around them, about conservation and about respecting nature and wildlife. It provides them with group social skills and teaches them to become more responsible and self-sufficient.

See p. 118 for recommended books on camping activities with kids.

Camping with babies

The following information has been provided by campingexpert.co.uk

Even the most enthusiastic camper might be put off by the thought of taking their baby on a camping trip. However, there is really no reason why your baby shouldn't join in the family fun. They will enjoy the change and will be fascinated by the different environment and all that nature has to offer. Camping with a baby does take a little more thought and preparation but for those who would like their child to grow up with an appreciation of the natural environment from a very young age, the extra effort will be very worthwhile.

Preparing for all kinds of weather

It is even more important to make adequate provision for all kinds of weather if you're taking a baby camping. Babies are unable to regulate their body temperature as well as adults so take extra warm clothes, hats and blankets. Conversely, if it's likely to be hot, take a portable fan so that your baby can keep cool more easily.

Your first time?

The first time you take your baby camping can be quite a daunting experience so if it's your first time, it may be a good idea to take them to a recreational campground where there are bound to be more facilities and you'll have easier access to help should anything go wrong.

Choose your campsite carefully

If your baby is not yet able to walk, try to choose a campsite where most of the land is flat. You're going to have to carry the baby most of the time when they are awake, so you don't want to be stumbling up and down steep banks with a baby in your arms. Neither do you want to be tumbling down rocks.

Don't worry about dirt!

It's the outdoors after all and the whole point of taking your baby on a camping trip is for them to experience nature. They'll love it. They'll want to be crawling through the dirt and they'll probably find lots of strange new things which they'll want to play with and even put in their mouth. Be vigilant at all times, of course, but don't worry if your baby gets a bit grubby. The fun they'll have will far outweigh any inconvenience a little dirt will cause. However, bringing along a playpen is a good idea as it will allow the baby to share the experience in a safe setting if you adults need a little chill-out time.

Carrying the baby

You will naturally have many responsibilities on a camping trip. It may be gathering wood for a fire, cooking the dinner, visiting the camp store and so on, so a baby backpack or front pack carrier is highly recommended. The front pack carrier option is even better for extremely young babies who might not have sufficiently developed head control muscles to be able to ride in a backpack. Carriers are great, especially if you plan to take a few hiking trips on your camping adventure and for keeping the baby safe as you go about your chores.

It's also a good idea to take a torch that can be worn around your head as you'll need to change nappies in the dark and may even want to carry your baby around after nightfall.

Animals, beasties and the Scottish midge!

Scotland's varied landscape and habitats means that there is a huge diversity of wildlife you may encounter.

Camping in Scotland often leads to direct contact with our best-known insect, the Scottish midge. The insect is tiny, just one or two millimetres in length, but it has a fearsome reputation, as the female is a bloodsucking insect with a bite. Generally the midge is found in higher numbers over the summer months and is most prevalent in the early morning and evening.

Bites from midges are irritating at the time and you can often see many of them on exposed skin. The insects are attracted by the carbon dioxide of expelled breath and recently this knowledge has been used to create midge machines which can attract and hoover up the insects on campsites and other outdoor venues. Midge bites have different effects on different people: some people have no physical reaction to their bites while others come out in blotches and others in rashes.

The midge's preferred habitats appear to be wherever there is damp ground and as a result it can be found extensively and in high numbers throughout the Highlands, especially after wet weather. Its range, however, is more significant than this; its territories extend far to the east and south of Scotland. There is a very good website www.midgeforecast.co.uk that predicts their levels in different areas.

Given that camping lends itself to getting close to nature and so unfortunately to midges there are some sensible precautions to take. By being prepared and well-informed you will be one step ahead and able to avoid the worst of any contact with them.

There are several creams and remedies on the market which claim to repel them; these include Smidge, from the same people responsible for the midge forecast, and Avon's Skin so Soft (available from Avon and from some outdoor shops). Please be aware that many of the insect repellents on the market cannot be used on children under a certain age so check the bottles carefully before you buy.

You can also prepare by having suitable clothing. A head net is a sensible precaution to take with you. It also helps if you are aware that midges are less prevalent in drier areas, do not like direct sunlight and tend not to fly in anything more than a very light breeze. This is well worth bearing in mind when picking your pitch as a damp pitch in total wind shelter, amongst trees and out of the sun will lead them to you first. Midges tend not to come indoors so often your safest option is to head inside when they begin to appear, but be advised to keep your insect netting closed as, like other insects, they can be attracted to a source of light at dusk.

There are other insects and bugs worth looking out for, with the tick the other main source of concern to those accessing the outdoors. Encounters with ticks are fairly rare for humans; they are more likely to end up on your dog. If you do take a dog on your camping trip it is always useful to check them every couple of days and remove any ticks at the earliest opportunity, using a specialist tick remover. Other supposedly effective methods of removing ticks (such as burning them or covering them in Vaseline or perfume) are certainly not recommended. Ticks are not nearly as prevalent as the midge; do bear in mind, however, that they are biting insects and they can and do remain attached to their blood source for several days, growing in size to that of a small pea. They can very occasionally transmit Lyme disease to humans. Ticks tend to be prevalent in areas where deer roam and will attach themselves to passing animals and humans (usually walking through long grass) before taking a bite. If you do notice a tick on your skin, it should be easy to remove it before it bites. Once attached, however, a tick remover may be needed to dislodge it as it is very important to remove the body and head together.

Scotland has no poisonous insects or spiders and so when taking children camping it is always useful to be prepared for a bit of beastie spotting. This opens up endless possibilities including pond dipping, rock pool exploring and insect safaris. Some kit may be required in terms of fishing nets and an insect viewer or insect peeper but this activity will keep kids entertained for hours – just remember to show them how to be responsible by putting the insects' and animals' homes and habitats back the way they found them afterwards.

There is one venomous snake in Scotland – the adder, which lives largely in rough open ground and is rarely encountered. Its main food sources are small mammals, frogs and toads. The adder is very shy and elusive and will only bite as a last defence – most people are bitten when they try to handle them. In the extremely unlikely event of coming across one, just leave it be.

There are no bears, wolves or other child-eating animals (as yet, at least) so you are at liberty to go on bear hunts and other such imaginary adventures.

Where can you camp in Scotland?

Camping trips involving tents, motorhomes and caravans have always been a popular way to experience Scotland. Drawn by the attractions of breathtaking beaches, glorious lochs and glens and magnificent mountains, both tourists and Scots themselves have found camping the best way to get back to nature and experience what Scotland has to offer close up.

Recent changes in legislation have changed the way you can camp in Scotland. In order to camp responsibly you should familiarise yourself with your rights and responsibilities before you pitch up.

The legislation is different according to the different types of camping, so do read carefully what the rules are, whether you are bringing a tent, a motorhome or a caravan.

Official campsites and caravan parks in Scotland offer a variety of facilities and experiences and there are hundreds to choose from. Unfortunately not all sites accept tents, motorhomes or caravans so do your research before setting off. Some sites may also have restrictions regarding the size of your group and the ages of group members and whether they accept pets. They are often fully booked during peak season so do contact them in advance and explain your requirements.

Scotland also has many 'unofficial' campsites. Generally these sites offer basic facilities which may include the use of public conveniences and a water tap. They are often run by community groups, estates or local crofting associations. You may be asked to pay a small fee or make a donation towards its upkeep. These sites can offer a slightly less basic alternative to roadside or wild camping.

Wild tent camping

Scotland's access legislation, contained within the Land Reform (Scotland) Act 2003, allows 'wild' tent camping on most unenclosed land. The Scottish Outdoor Access Code gives guidance and practical advice and states that this form of tent camping must be done responsibly and it is the campers' responsibility to leave no trace.

The Scottish Outdoor Access Code advises that 'Access rights extend to wild camping. This type of camping is lightweight, done in small numbers and only for two or three nights in any one place. You can camp in this way wherever access rights apply but help to avoid causing problems for local people and land managers by not camping in enclosed fields of crops or farm animals and by keeping well away from buildings, roads or historic structures. Take extra care to avoid disturbing deer stalking or grouse shooting. If you wish to camp close to a house or building, seek the owner's permission'.

Leave no trace by:

- taking away all your litter

- removing all traces of your tent pitch and any open fire (follow the guidance for lighting fires)

- not causing any pollution.

The Code describes responsible behaviour with respect to wild camping, as defined above. Camping has, however, traditionally taken place in many other places, including relatively accessible road or lochside sites. Camping in these places is lawful and may have few adverse effects, and can indeed provide a relatively safe and accessible introduction to this activity for the young or inexperienced. Such locations can be very prominent and may attract frequent use.

Campers therefore need to take extra care to avoid harming the environment or causing problems for local residents. The Scottish National Access Forum has identified a number of key messages for campers which are particularly relevant to these situations:

- Avoid overcrowding by moving on to another location.

- Carry a trowel to bury your human waste and urinate well away from open water, rivers and burns.

- Use a stove or leave no trace of any campfire. Never cut down or damage trees.

- Take away your rubbish and consider picking up other litter as well.

- If in doubt, ask the landowner. Following their advice may help you find a better camping spot.

- Access rights are not an excuse for anti-social or illegal behaviour.

Further information on wild camping can be gained from the following websites: www.outdooraccess-scotland.com and www.mcofs.org.uk

Guidance for camping wild with campervans and motorhomes in Scotland

Several campervan and motorhome rental companies have collaborated to create the Campervan and Motorhome Professional Association (CaMPA) and have produced these simple, common sense guidelines about camping wild with campervans and motorhomes in Scotland. It is important to note that access legislation relevant to tent campers does not relate to caravan and motorhome users. The guidance about camping wild with campervans and motorhomes is as follows:

Access rights

Scotland is rightly proud of its access rights; however when you're looking for places to camp wild in a campervan or motorhome, it is important to bear in mind the following key points:

- Scottish access rights and the Scottish Outdoor Access Code don't apply to motor vehicles.

- The Road Traffic Act 1988 states that you can drive a vehicle up to 15 yards off a public road for the purposes of parking, but this does not confer any right to park the vehicle, nor to stay there overnight. Most unmetalled roads, unfenced land and beaches are private property, and you don't have the right to park unless it's authorised by the landowner by verbal agreement or signage.

- In practice, informal off-road parking takes place in many parts of rural Scotland, often in well-established places, without causing undue concern.

- Some communities (eg Calgary Bay on Mull, and the whole island of Tiree) have established their own guidance for campervans and the use of designated overnight parking spaces... if you're in such a place, follow the guidance!

Common sense guidance – do:

- use common sense and think whether the spot you have found is suitable for a vehicle.

- think about the cumulative effect of camping in the 'fantastic secret place which I'm sure no one else has ever been'... it is very likely that others will use the same spot, not just you!

- take great care to avoid fragile ground/sensitive habitats (eg wild flower-rich machair on the Western Isles) – never drive down to beaches or onto grass verges as it destroys the habitat.

- avoid over-crowding. If another vehicle is parked in a secluded spot, try not to park right next to it and find your own spot elsewhere.

- use only biodegradable detergents and drain kitchen waste water tanks in campsites at designated areas. If your tank has to be emptied in the wild, keep away from watercourses and be aware that animals will be attracted to the scent.

- carry a trowel to bury any human waste and urinate well away from open water, rivers and burns. Toilet paper should be bagged and taken away with you – not buried (animals dig it up).

- do a full 'litter-pick' before you leave, taking all your rubbish, and any you found there already, and disposing of it properly when you're back in 'civilisation'.

- support a sustainable tourism industry – buy groceries in local shops.

Common sense guidance – don't:

- park in areas where signs state 'No overnight parking'.

- park overnight within sight of people's houses, even in car park bays.

- block access tracks to estates and fields.

- light BBQs or fires unless it is safe to do so, and you can supervise it properly. They should be fully extinguished when finished and no evidence left behind.

- empty any chemical toilet waste anywhere other than at a designated chemical waste area. The majority of campsites have facilities for emptying a cassette toilet. Most public toilets are not suitable places to empty chemical toilets, as it upsets the sewage treatment process.

ScottishCamping.com acknowledges CaMPA (campa.org.uk).

BE A
RESPONSIBLE
CAMPER

The Scottish Outdoor Access Code provides advice about how to camp responsibly in Scotland.

LIGHTING FIRES. Never cut down or damage trees. Use a stove if possible. If you must have an open fire keep it small and under control and remove all traces before leaving.

TOILET WASTE. If public toilets aren't available, carry a trowel and bury your own waste and urinate well away from open water, rivers and burns.

LITTER. Take away all your rubbish and consider picking up other litter as well.

Visit **outdooraccess-scotland.com** or contact your local Scottish Natural Heritage office.

KNOW THE CODE
BEFORE YOU GO

SCOTTISH
OUTDOOR ACCESS CODE   outdooraccess-scotland.com

Environmental camping

What is the cost of your camping trip on the environment?

Did you know that thousands of tents are discarded each year after festivals or camping trips? Despite some organisations trying to encourage the reuse of leftover tents, many continue to be dumped in landfill sites. Scotland has many great places to camp and some of the most liberal rules relating to camping in Europe. Are you aware that the Scottish Outdoor Access Code states that it is your responsibility to protect the environment while camping? Can you spend a little time thinking about your impact on the environment to protect it for the generations to come?

What is the real cost of your equipment?

Before buying any equipment do you consider the alternatives? Do you think about the materials used to produce the equipment and whether they are sustainable and recyclable? Were you aware that aluminium poles are more easily recycled than fibreglass? What about cotton, canvas and nylon? If you decide to buy then think about the quality and likely lifetime of your new tent and equipment. A quality tent is likely to outlast several cheap ones. They are made to keep out the elements, could save you money in the long run and are more likely to prevent that soggy sleeping bag. Is it possible for you to consider borrowing or renting a tent as an alternative?

Open fire, BBQ or stove?

What effects do different fuel types have on the environment? Can you give some thought as to the materials used in the production of your stove, the sustainability of your fuel type and the possibilities of using alternatives? You may reduce the impact of your camping. Do you know what a fire pan is and how to use one? Petrol, gas and other oil-based fuels come at a cost from their production methods, transportation and resultant CO_2 emissions.

Driftwood and many naturally regenerating wood sources can provide an alternative source of fuel to petrochemical fuel types. In some circumstances small, well-managed wood fires can provide an alternative but they must be managed appropriately.

Disposable BBQs are not considered environmentally sound but if you do use one can you reduce its impact by recycling the metal components along with any other waste products from your trip?

What would happen if everyone considered their impact on the environment and followed the advice on responsible camping contained within the Scottish Outdoor Access Code. Could it lead to less use of the following?

Recipes

Mains

Corned beef hash
Ingredients:

Tatties

Eggs

Tin of corned beef

Mustard

Cheese

Butter

Method:

1) Boil the tatties in the pot and add a couple of eggs before completing the boil.
2) Whilst the potatoes are boiling, chop the corned beef into cubes and grate the cheese.
3) When the eggs are hard boiled, peel and chop them.
4) Mash the tatties with the butter and then add the corned beef, the mustard and the chopped hard-boiled eggs.
5) Mash and mix everything together before sprinkling with the cheese.
6) Serve and enjoy.

Submitted by Alex Barclay from Scotland

Creamy mushroom pasta

Ingredients:

Pasta

Tin of condensed mushroom soup (or experiment with different soups; you can't go wrong)

Method:

1) Boil up some pasta.
2) When ready drain.
3) Stir in condensed mushroom soup.
4) Serve and enjoy.

Submitted by Kenny Lyne from Aberdeenshire

Easy pasta meal

Ingredients:

Your favourite pasta

Packet of cheese sauce mix

Tin of peppered spam or a smoked sausage

Broccoli (optional)

Method:

1) Boil up the pasta and the broccoli, if you want some veg with this (you can do this in the same pan).
2) Just before it's ready make up the cheese sauce and chop the peppered spam or smoked sausage into small batons.
3) Drain the pasta and then mix everything in the pan.
4) Serve immediately with crusty bread.

Submitted by Daisy from Central Scotland

Quick chilli

Ingredients:

An onion

A few cloves of garlic

Tin of corned beef

Tin of tomatoes

Tin of baked beans

Chilli powder or chilli sauce

Oil

Rice or crusty bread to serve

Method:

1) Slice the onion and fry in oil then chop the garlic and add it to the pan.

2) Throw in your chopped corned beef, tomatoes and baked beans.

3) Add chilli to taste and warm through for five minutes or so.

4) Serve with boiled rice or crusty bread. You can omit the onion and garlic if desired.

Submitted by April Shower's

Chilli

I am a regular camper with my boyfriend and find that if you are only camping for one or two nights, a good idea is to cook some meals such as chilli and rice before you go and simply keep them cool and then heat them up on the fire (in foil) or on a stove (in a pot) and that will give you a filling cooked meal! It's a very effective way not to go hungry and makes your camping trip more enjoyable because you don't have to worry about cooking!

Submitted by Karen from Glasgow

Pesto pasta

Ingredients:

Pasta

A tin of sweetcorn or peas

A jar of pesto

A tin of tuna or salmon

Grated cheese

Method:

1) Boil the pasta and just before it's done add a tin of drained sweetcorn or peas to heat them through.

2) Drain the pasta and sweetcorn/peas.

3) Add the jar of pesto and a tin or two of drained tuna or salmon and give it all a good stir.

4) Top with the grated cheese.

Submitted by Cheryl from Cardiff

Splash 'n' pinch beef stew

Ingredients:

A large tin of corned beef (chopped)

A large tin of oxtail soup

Two small tins of mixed vegetables (drained)

A small tin of potatoes (drained)

A large splash of Worcester sauce

A large pinch of dried mixed herbs

Salt and pepper to taste

Method:

1) Mix all the ingredients in a saucepan, heat through and serve with crusty bread.

Submitted by Noble Gomes from Middlesbrough

Aussie outback hobo dinner

Ingredients:

4 medium potatoes, peeled and sliced

Half a medium onion, diced

1 lb (500g) mince

A quarter of a cup of water

Salt and pepper to taste

Ketchup to serve

Aluminium foil

Method:

1) Add the water to the mince and mix well.
2) Add the potatoes, onion and seasoning. Mix well.
3) Separate into three or four servings.
4) Wrap in double-thickness aluminium foil.
5) Place seam side up on a medium hot grill or open fire and cook for 40 minutes, turning often.
6) Open carefully and serve with ketchup.

Submitted by David Gray from Barrhead, Glasgow

Pomping stew
Ingredients:
A tin of chunky steak

A tin of Scotch Broth or oxtail soup

A tin of carrots

A tin of potatoes

Method:
1) Put everything in a pan, simmer through until heated thoroughly. Add salt and pepper to taste.

Submitted by Ian from Lancashire

Spicy sausage with ginger
Ingredients:
Sausages

Pasta

Onions, chopped

Garlic, chopped

Oregano

Powdered ginger

Jar of pasta sauce

Garlic oil

Method:
1) Fry the sausage, onions and garlic.
2) Add the ginger, stir well, then add the jar of sauce.
3) Meanwhile, boil the pasta. When ready, drain and add to the sausage mix.
4) Stir well and simmer for a couple of minutes until piping hot.

Submitted by Archie McBride from Glasgow

Quick and snazzy chasseur (on a single stove)

One for adults only...

Ingredients:

A small baggy of gravy browning

A beef stock cube

A small bottle wine (you only need a small dash for the sauce)

A piece of sirloin or fillet steak

A couple of tomatoes, chopped

A couple of mushrooms

A frying pan or small pot

Method:

1) Pre-boil the water and store it in a cup flask.
2) Cut the steak into thin slices and fry it off.
3) When the steak is nearly cooked add the tomatoes and hot water.
4) Mix the gravy browning and stock cube with some hot water into a paste and add gradually to the pan until you get your desired consistency.
5) Add a dash of vino.
6) Serve and enjoy.

Submitted by 2 folk and a Northface Chat and a dug

Ragin' risotto

Another for the adults only ... this should serve two.

Ingredients:

A vegetable stock cube

An onion, sliced

Two cloves of garlic, chopped or crushed

150g rice

1/3 glass wine

Oil

Cheese

Salt and pepper

Crusty bread

Method:

1) Make a pint of veggie stock with the stock cube and water. Bring it to the boil.
2) Take the stock off the heat and heat the oil in a pan.
3) Fry the sliced onion until it begins to soften. Add the garlic and mix up like a DJ on the proverbial.
4) Add the rice and stir for a minute (until glistening and, well, nice-looking), then add the wine.
5) Over the next 20 minutes continue to heat and incrementally add the stock as it becomes absorbed, reserving about half a glass of stock at the end.
6) Finally, add the rest of the stock, a pinch of salt and pepper to taste.
7) Serve with crusty bread for a double carb hit and add cheese until the cheeseometer hits at least a '7'.

Submitted by Phil S from Derbyshire

Puddings

Choc chip custard dessert
Ingredients:
Packet of instant custard
Packet of choc-chip cookies

Method:
1) Use boiling water to make up the instant custard – one sachet for every two people.
2) Roughly crumble the choc-chip cookies into the custard – use up to half a packet per custard sachet.
3) Stir well and serve up!

Submitted by Marina from Strathkinness, Fife

Hot apples
Ingredients:
One apple per person
Sultanas and/or raisins
Sugar (brown is best)
Tin foil

Method:
1) Core the apples.
2) Fill the centre of each apple with sultanas, raisins and sugar.
3) Wrap the apples in tin foil.
4) Put next to the fire or in hot embers for 15–20 minutes.
5) Take out of the fire and unwrap (use sticks as the parcels will be hot!).
6) Serve and enjoy.

Submitted by David from Newcastle

Bonkers bananas

Ingredients:

One banana per person

One pack chocolate buttons for every two people

Cream

Tin foil

Method:

1) Carefully slit bananas (still in their skins) along the inside curve.
2) Push in as many chocolate buttons as possible.
3) Wrap in tin foil.
4) Put on the fire or barbeque until the skins go black and the bananas are soft.
5) Serve with cream.

Submitted by Puckbunny from Stonehaven

Hot peaches

Ingredients:

Peaches

Brown sugar or jam

Method:

1) Cut the peaches in half and add brown sugar or a spoonful of jam to the hole where the stone was.
2) Wrap the peaches carefully in foil keeping them right side up.
3) Put into the embers and heat for 5–10 mins – yummy served with ice cream.

Submitted by Fran from Edinburgh

Snacks

Drop scones
Ingredients:
250g self-raising flour
4tsp sugar
2 eggs
½ pint milk
Butter

Method:
1) Mix all the ingredients together. If you can whisk the mixture, so much the better, but getting rid of lumps will suffice.
2) Melt a small bit of butter in a hot frying pan and ladle tablespoonfuls of the mixture in.
3) Turn the drop scones when a few bubbles appear and cook the other side.
4) Pass to the inevitable waiting hungry crowd. They can be eaten as they are, or with a range of yummy stuff on top.

Submitted by Alison Garnett from Oxon

Books for camping with kids

Heather Amery and Stephen Cartwright, *Camping Out (Farmyard Tales Sticker Storybooks)* (Usborne Publishing, 2005)

Heather Amery and Stephen Cartwright, *Camping Out (Mini Farmyard Tales)* (Usborne Publishing, 2005)

Lucy Cousins, *Maisy Goes Camping* (Walker Books Ltd, 2005)

Fiona Danks and Jo Schofield, *Make It Wild! 101 Things To Make And Do Outdoors* (Frances Lincoln, 2010)

Ladybird, *Peppa Pig: Peppa Goes Camping* (Ladybird Books, 2010)

Nickelodeon, *Dora's Camping Trip (Dora the Explorer)* (Simon and Schuster, 2008)

Jeremy Strong, *My Brother's Famous Bottom Goes Camping* (Puffin, 2008)

Jo Schofield and Fiona Danks, *Go Wild! 101 Things To Do Outdoors Before You Grow Up* (Frances Lincoln, 2009)

Acknowledgements

Andrew Thomson and ScottishCamping.com would like to acknowledge the contributions by Vango, who provided images and information on camping equipment, and www.campingexpertco.uk, who contributed information on camping with babies, camping activities for kids and what to know before you go camping.

We also wish to acknowledge Big Tree Campervans (www.bigtreecampervans.com) for their assistance with campervan- and motorhome-related matters.

Photographs

Photograph on p. 60 © Iain Cameron
Camping equipment images p. 77 © Vango
Camping stove images p. 81 © Trangia
Scotland Campsites and Caravan Parks Map p. 120 © Iain Cameron

Images on front cover are (left to right):
Loch Morlich at Glenmore Camping and Caravanning Site
Comrie Croft Eco Camping
Sands Caravan and Camping Park

Back cover top are (left to right):
Clachtoll Beach Campsite
Beeswing Caravan Park
Author's campervan at Carradale Bay

Back cover bottom are (left to right):
Shieling Holidays
Cannich Caravan and Camping Site
Hoddom Castle

p. iii Yellowcraig Broad Sands
pp. iv and v Sands Caravan and Camping Park
pp. 6 and 7 Sands Caravan and Camping Park
pp. 68 and 69 Clachtoll Beach Campsite
pp. 70 and 71 Top Glenmore Camping and Caravanning Site
Bottom Carradale Bay
p. 72 Kippford Holiday Park
p. 84 Glenmore Camping and Caravanning Site
p. 87 Carradale Bay Caravan Park
p. 88 Kippford Holiday Park
p. 94 No location identified
p. 97 Clachtoll Beach Campsite
p. 98 Wild camping at Glen Pean
p. 106 No Camping sign near Glen Lyon, Perthshire

Scotland Campsites and Caravan Parks Map

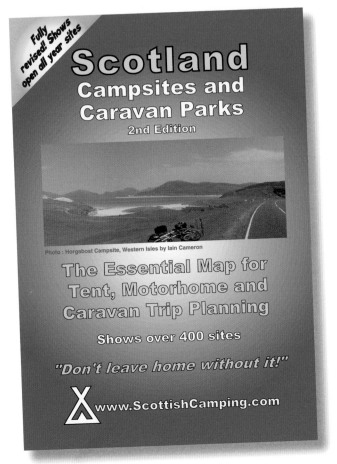

The essential map for tent, motorhome
and caravan trip planning.
Shows over 400 sites.

"Don't leave home without it!"